Super Scary
HALLOWEEN CROCHET

Super Scary
HALLOWEEN CROCHET

35 GRUESOME PATTERNS TO SINK YOUR HOOK INTO

NICKI TRENCH

CICO BOOKS

LONDON NEW YORK

This edition published in 2017 by CICO Books
An imprint of Ryland Peters & Small Ltd
20–21 Jockey's Fields   341 E 116th St
London WC1R 4BW   New York, NY 10029

www.rylandpeters.com

First published in 2011 by CICO Books under the title *Super Scary Crochet*

10 9 8 7 6 5 4 3 2 1

Text © Nicki Trench 2011
Design, illustration, and photography © CICO Books 2011

A CIP catalog record for this book is available from the Library of Congress and the British Library.

ISBN: 978 1 78249 469 0

Printed in China

Editor: Marie Clayton
Designers: Paul Tilby and Jacqui Caulton
Photographer: Claire Richardson
Illustrator: Stephen Dew
Stylist: Rob Merrett
Pattern checker: Beryl Oakes

In-house editor: Anna Galkina
Art director: Sally Powell
Head of production: Patricia Harrington
Publishing manager: Penny Craig
Publisher: Cindy Richards

CONTENTS

INTRODUCTION

Making the Super Scaries has been a scream. The whole process has been like bringing up children; you never know what you're going to get! It has been impossible to plan the characters (how could you know exactly how Bigfoot would turn out with all his fur?), but there has been plenty of inspiration from the TV and big screen for toys such as Dominic the Vampire, Dr Death, and my own personal favorite, the Pocket Ghost.

The wool I've used is mostly light worsted (double knitting), which is a good standard thickness and comes in a variety of colors. The toys use very little yarn—most use half a 1¾oz ball and a couple of scraps for details, so they are very cheap to make. The hook sizes vary, but most use a standard F/5 (4mm) size hook. All the necessary information is stated in each pattern.

Most of the toys are crocheted in the round in spirals using a stitch marker, which is placed in the loop on the hook at the beginning of each round. You can buy all sorts of fancy stitch markers, but I find it easier to use a contrast-colored piece of yarn about 3in (7.5cm) long. I highly recommend using a stitch marker—it may take a little more time but the results are worth it.

The secret of getting the character of the toys is in the detail. Feel free to bring your own sense of horror as you make them or customize them to resemble family or friends. Some of the details on the toys can be dangerous—for example, Piercing Phyllis has pins in her hair and hands. The eyes used are generally 9mm safety eyes (use only these if you plan to give a toy to a small child), but some are simply embroidered or flat-backed beads stuck on with a strong adhesive.

Stuffing is an important part of making a toy. Add a small piece at a time to mold the toy into shape and never over-stuff; these toys are supposed to be squishy and cuddly despite their appearance. If you want them to stand up, put more stuffing in the legs. You can buy different-colored stuffing; use a dark brown/black stuffing for darker toys and white for the lighter ones.

The hair is also key to giving your toy character, so spend time getting the shaping right. I usually start from the hairline and then fill in the spaces around the head. Most of the hair is made using the same method as making tassels—by cutting a strip of yarn, folding it in half, threading the loop through the crochet with a hook, threading the tails of the strand through the loop, and pulling to secure. Another method is to cut several strands and lay them horizontally across the head, then secure down by giving the toy a center parting using a back stitch.

Also included is a wonderful techniques section to cover the stitches used in this book. Most of the toys are made using single crochet, which is the most basic of stitches. If you haven't crocheted in the round before, give it a go, but don't forget to practice using the stitch marker.

CROCHET STITCH CONVERSION CHART

Crochet stitches are worked in the same way in both the USA and the UK, but the stitch names are not the same and identical names are used for different stitches. Below is a list of the US terms used in this book, and the equivalent UK terms.

US TERM	UK TERM
single crochet (sc)	double crochet (dc)
half double crochet (hdc)	half treble (htr)
double crochet (dc)	treble (tr)
treble (tr)	double treble (dtr)
double treble (dtr)	triple treble (trtr)
triple treble (trtr)	quadruple treble (qtr)
gauge	tension
yarn over hook (yoh)	yarn round hook (yrh)

CHAPTER 1
SCARY FAMILIES

Meet a different kind of Mummy who most certainly won't cook you dinner. The Queen of The Vampires' favorite snack is your blood, but she wouldn't want to eat the oven-roasted rat Baby Jane has made for Blanche's lunch. Don't be scared when the Pocket Ghost announces his arrival to your family and make sure you pay a visit to Mr & Mrs Alien and their brood.

MATERIALS

Pure wool light worsted (DK) yarn:

Head, Body, Hands: ½ × 1¾oz (50g) ball—approx 62yd (56.5m)—of off-white (A)

Legs, Arms, Eyebrows, Hair: ½ × 1¾oz (50g) ball—approx 62yd (56.5m)—of black (B)

Shoes: Small amount of purple (C)

Mouth: Scrap of red (D)

Eye surrounds: Small piece gray felt

Safety eyes

Fiberfill stuffing

Bodice: Small piece black felt, purple embroidery floss

Fangs: Small piece white felt

Crown: Small piece gold felt, purple sequins

Underskirt: Approx 8 × 8in (20 × 20cm) satin or light cotton fabric

Overskirt: Approx 4½ × 14in (11.5 × 35.5cm) lace or netting

Crochet hook size: E/4 (3.5mm)

ABBREVIATIONS

Ch chain

Rep repeat

Sc single crochet

Sc2tog *insert hook into next st and draw up a loop; rep from * once, yarn over, draw through all 3 loops on hook.

Ss slip stitch

St(s) stitch(es)

SIZE

Approx height: 8in (21cm)

QUEEN LUCY OF THE VAMPIRES

The Queen is a very, very old woman vampire who is posing as a beautiful young teenage girl—like all vampires, she is immortal. Over many centuries she has developed an unquenchable blood thirst for fit young teenage boys who like to play baseball and basketball.

HEAD

Using A, make 2ch, 6sc in second ch from hook.

Round 1: 2sc in each st. (12 sts)

Round 2: *1sc in next st, 2sc in next st; rep from * to end of round. (18 sts)

Round 3: *1sc in each of next 2 sts, 2sc in next st; rep from * to end of round. (24 sts)

Rounds 4–8: 1sc in each st.

Round 9: *1sc in each of next 2 sts, sc2tog; rep from * to end of round. (18 sts)

Round 10: *1sc in next st, sc2tog; rep from * to end of round. (12 sts)

Cut two small circles in gray felt. Cut a hole in the middle of each, insert safety eyes and push into position in face. Stuff head.

Round 11: Sc2tog until opening is closed. Fasten off.

BODY

Using A, make 2ch, 6sc in second ch from hook.

Round 1: 2sc in each st. (12 sts)

Round 2: *1sc into next st, 2sc into next st; rep from * to end of round. (18 sts)

Rounds 3–11: 1sc in each st.

Stuff lightly.

Round 12: *1sc into next st, sc2tog; rep from * to end of round. (12 sts)

Round 13: Sc2tog until opening is closed. Fasten off.

SHOES & LEGS (make 2)

Using C, make 2ch, 6sc in second ch from hook.

Round 1: *1sc in next st, 2sc in next st; rep from * to end of round. (9 sts)

Rounds 2–4: 1sc in each st.

Change to B.

Cont making 1sc in each st until leg measures approx 3in (8cm).

Fasten off.

ARMS (make 2)

Using A, make 2ch, 5sc in second ch from hook.

Round 1: *1sc in next st, 2sc in next st; rep from * once, 1sc in last st. (7 sts)

Rounds 2–3: 1sc in each st.

Change to B.

Cont making 1sc in each st until arm measures approx 2½in (6cm).

Fasten off.

MAKING UP

Pin and sew body to head. Stuff legs and arms and pin and sew to body. Embroider mouth using D. Cut two small diamonds of white felt for fangs and hand sew using thread at each side of mouth. Embroider eyebrows using B.

HAIR

Using B, wrap yarn round a book, CD, or DVD case approx 10 times, then cut along one side. Lay strands of yarn across head at front and attach by sewing small back stitches, using B and a tapestry/wool sewing needle. Repeat until strands of yarn cover front and back of head. Fill in gaps by threading individual strands through head, looping yarn through stitches and threading tails and then pulling tight to secure in place.

CROWN

Measure circumference of doll's head and cut a strip of yellow/gold felt to size and approx 1in (2.5cm) wide. Cut out crown shape, hand sew sequins, and sew in place onto doll's head.

BODICE

Using the template on page 109, place the marked edge on a fold and cut bodice from black felt. Sew into place on doll. Embroider two crosses using purple embroidery floss.

SKIRT

UNDER SKIRT

Cut a 7½in (19cm) diameter circle. Cut another circle from the middle to match waist size of doll. Pull legs through hole and hand sew skirt around doll's waist.

LACE OUTER SKIRT

Hand sew the short edges of the length of lace together using running stitch. Turn right side out. Make a row of running stitch approx ¼in (0.5cm) from the top long edge. Place outer skirt onto doll and pull thread ends to gather skirt to fit waist. Stitch in place. Cut length to size if necessary.

POCKET GHOST

This little ghost loves haunting pockets—the warmth and darkness give him comfort—but he can give people quite a shock when they find him inside unexpectedly. Watch out, he may be in yours!

MATERIALS

Pure wool light worsted (DK) yarn:
Head, Body, Arms, Legs: ½ × 1¾oz (50g) ball—approx 62yd (56.5m)—of cream
Safety eyes
Fiberfill stuffing
Mouth: Black yarn
Cape: Piece white cotton fabric
Crochet hook size: F/5 (4mm)

ABBREVIATIONS

Ch chain
Rep repeat
Sc single crochet
Sc2tog *insert hook into next st and draw up a loop; rep from * once, yarn over, draw through all 3 loops on hook.
Ss slip stitch
St(s) stitch(es)

SIZE

Approx height: 5¼in (13cm)

HEAD

Make 2ch, 6sc in second chain from hook.
Round 1: 2sc in each st. (12 sts)
Round 2: *1sc in next st, 2sc in next st; rep from * to end of round. (18 sts)
Round 3: *1sc in next 2 sts, 2sc in next st; rep from * to end of round. (24 sts)
Rounds 4–10: 1sc in each st. (24 sts)
Round 11: *1sc in next 2 sts, sc2tog; rep from * to end of round. (18 sts)
Round 12: 1sc in each st. (18 sts)
Round 13: *1sc in next st, sc2tog; rep from * to end of round. (12 sts)
Fasten off.

BODY

Make 2ch, 6sc in second chain from hook.
Round 1: 2sc in each st. (12 sts)
Round 2: *1sc, 2sc in next st; rep from * to end of round. (18 sts)
Rounds 3–10: 1sc in each st.
Round 11: *1sc in first st, sc2tog; rep from * to end of round. (12 sts)
Fasten off.

ARMS (make 2)

Make 2ch, 6sc in second chain from hook.
Rounds 1–5: 1sc in each st.
Fasten off, leaving a long tail.

LEGS (make 2)

Make 2ch, 6sc in second chain from hook.
Rounds 1–4: 1sc in each st.
Fasten off, leaving a long tail.

MAKING UP

Sew in ends. Insert safety eyes and stuff head firmly. Stuff body, pin and sew to head. Pin and sew arms and legs to body (do not stuff). Sew mouth in black yarn.

CAPE

Cut a piece of white cotton fabric 4 × 8in (10 × 20cm). Make a small hem along each side. Gather the top and hand sew around neck.

BABY JANE AND BLANCHE

Baby Jane hates her sister, Blanche. She pushed her down the stairs and then fed her on rats for days. Blanche hates Baby Jane too—once she tried to run her over, but Baby Jane survived. So the two sisters are destined to live out the rest of their lives in hatefulness.

MATERIALS

Pure wool light worsted (DK) yarn:
Body, Head, Arms, Legs: ½ × 1¾oz (50g) ball—approx 62yd (56.5m)—of cream (A)
Shoes: Small amount of deep pink (B)
Hair: ¼ × 1¾oz (50g) ball—approx 31yd (28.5m)—of yellow (C)
Dress: ¼ × 1¾oz (50g) ball—approx 31yd (28.5m)—of pale pink (D)
Rat: Small amount of brown (E)
Safety eyes
Fiberfill stuffing
Eyelashes, Eyebrows: Black floss
Mouth: Scrap red yarn
Small piece of pink ribbon
Crochet hook size: F/5 (4mm)

ABBREVIATIONS

Beg beginning
Ch chain
Dc double crochet
Rep repeat
Sc single crochet
Sc2tog *insert hook into next st and draw up a loop; rep from * once, yarn over, draw through all 3 loops on hook.
Sc3tog *insert hook into next st and draw up a loop; rep from * twice, yarn over, draw through all 4 loops on hook.
Ss slip stitch
St(s) stitch(es)

SIZE

Approx height: 8in (21cm)

BABY JANE

HEAD

Using A, make 2ch, 6sc in second ch from hook.
Round 1: 2sc in each st. (12 sts)
Round 2: *1sc in next st, 2sc in next st; rep from * to end of round. (18 sts)
Round 3: *1sc in each of next 2 sts, 2sc in next st; rep from * to end of round. (24 sts)
Rounds 4–8: 1sc in each st.
Round 9: *1sc in each of next 2 sts, sc2tog; rep from * to end of round. (18 sts)
Round 10: *1sc in next st, sc2tog; rep from * to end of round. (12 sts)
Insert safety eyes and stuff head.
Round 11: Sc2tog until opening is closed.
Fasten off.

BODY

Using A, make 2ch, 6sc in second ch from hook.
Round 1: 2sc in each st. (12 sts)
Round 2: *1sc into next st, 2sc into next st; rep from * to end of round. (18 sts)
Rounds 3–11: 1sc in each st.
Stuff lightly.
Round 12: *1sc into next st, sc2tog; rep from * to end of round. (12 sts)
Round 13: Sc2tog until opening is closed.
Fasten off.

SHOES & LEGS (make 2)

Using B, make 2ch, 6sc in second ch from hook.
Round 1: *1sc in next st, 2sc in next st; rep from * to end of round. (9 sts)
Rounds 2–4: 1sc in each st.
Change to A.
Round 5: Sc2tog, 1sc in each st to end of round. (8 sts)
Rounds 6–12: 1sc in each st.
Fasten off.

ARMS (make 2)

Using A, make 2ch, 5sc in second ch from hook.
Round 1: *1sc in next st, 2sc in next st; rep from * once, 1sc in last st. (7 sts)
Rounds 2–9: 1sc in each st.
Fasten off.

MAKING UP

Pin and sew body to head. Stuff, pin, and sew legs to body. Stuff, pin, and sew arms to body. Sew one arm slightly raised to hold rat. Embroider mouth, eyebrows, and eyelashes.

HOLLYWOOD 'WHAT EVER HAPPENED
PRODUCTION TO BABY JANE'
DIRECTOR ROBERT ALDRICH
CAMERA ERNEST HALLER

DATE	SCENE	TAKE
1962	3	2

HAIR

Hair is made using 2 strands of loops. Using C, *make enough chain to stretch from ear to ear. Mark end of foundation row with a st marker. Make an additional 40ch beyond marked st, then ss into ch next to marker.
**Make 40ch, ss into next ch of foundation chain. Cont from ** until end of row.
Fasten off. *

Attach hair to front of Jane's head, styling as you go. Place st in center for center parting. Bunch up a little hair on each side of parting.
Rep from * to * once more, attaching second strand behind first to give hair volume.
Make a bow and tie in center of parting at front.

DRESS

Using D, make 30ch, ss in first ch to form a ring.
Rounds 1–4: 1sc in each st. (30 sts)
Round 5: Sc2tog, 1sc in each of next 14 sts, sc2tog, 1sc in each st to end of round. (28 sts)
Round 6: Sc2tog, 1sc in each of next 13 sts, sc2tog, 1sc in each st to end of round. (26 sts)
Round 7: 1sc in each st.
Round 8: Sc2tog, 1sc in each of next 12 sts, sc2tog, 1sc in each st to end of round. (24 sts)
Round 9: Sc2tog, 1sc in each of next 11 sts, sc2tog, 1sc in each st to last st, ss to first st. (22 sts)
Fasten off.

Bottom of dress:

Turn dress upside down, join yarn at start of round.
Round 1: 2sc in first st, 1sc in each of next 14 sts, 2sc in next st, 1sc in each st to end of round. (32 sts)
Round 2: 2sc in first st, 1sc in each of next 15 sts, 2sc in next st, 1sc in each st to end of round. (34 sts)
Rounds 3–5: 1sc in each st, ending last round ss in first st.

Round 6: *skip 1 st, 5dc into next st; rep from * to end, ss in last st.
Fasten off.

Left shoulder:

Turn dress right way up and work shoulders. With fasten-off point on your right, join yarn in third st in towards center.
Row 1: 1sc in each of next 3 sts, turn. (3 sts)
Row 2: 1sc in each of next 2 sts, turn. (2 sts)
Row 3: Sc2tog, turn. (1 st)
Row 4: 1sc in st, turn.
Row 5: 2sc in st, turn. (2 sts)
Row 6: 1sc in each of next 2 sts, turn. (2 sts)
Row 7: 2sc in next st, 1sc in next st. (3 sts)
Fasten off.

Right shoulder:

Leave 3 sts free after left shoulder, join yarn to next st and work as left shoulder.
Try dress on doll, pin and sew straps in place to back of dress.

RAT

Work in rows.
Using E, make 5ch, 1sc in last ch, turn.
Row 1: 8sc into first st. (8 sts)
Row 2: 1ch, 1sc in each st.
Rows 3–4: 1ch, 1sc to end.
Row 5: Sc2tog, 1sc in each st to last 2 sts, sc2tog. (6 sts)
Row 6: Sc2tog to end. (3 sts)
Row 7: Sc2tog, 1sc in last st. (2 sts)
Row 8: 2sc in first st, 1sc in next st. (3 sts)
Row 9: 2sc in first st, 1sc in next st, 2sc in last st. (5 sts)
Row 10: Sc2tog twice, 1sc. (3 sts)
Row 11: Sc3tog.
Fasten off.
Sew rat together lengthways. Make French knots for ears and legs. Sew onto Baby Jane's raised arm.

BLANCHE

MATERIALS

Pure wool light worsted (DK) yarn:
Head, Body, Legs: ½ × 1¾oz (50g) ball —approx 62yd (56.5m)—of beige (A)
Arms, Dress: ¼ × 1¾oz (50g) ball —approx 31yd (28.5m)—of deep green (B)
Mouth, Hair: Small amount of dark brown (C)
Safety eyes
Fiberfill stuffing
Eyelashes, Eyebrows: Black embroidery floss
Scarf: 20in (50cm) ribbon or chiffon
Crochet hook size: F/5 (4mm)

SIZE

Approx height: 9in (23cm)

HEAD

Using A, make 2ch, 6sc in second ch from hook.
Round 1: 2sc in each st. (12 sts)
Round 2: *1sc in next st, 2sc in next st; rep from * to end of round. (18 sts)
Round 3: *1sc in each of next 2 sts, 2sc in next st; rep from * to end of round. (24 sts)
Rounds 4–8: 1sc in each st.
Round 9: *1sc in next 2 sts, sc2tog; rep from * to end of round. (18 sts)
Round 10: *1sc in next st, sc2tog; rep from * to end of round. (12 sts)
Insert safety eyes and stuff head.
Round 11: Sc2tog until opening is closed.
Fasten off.

BODY

Using A, make 2ch, 6sc in second ch from hook.
Round 1: 2sc in each st. (12 sts)
Round 2: *1sc into next st, 2sc into next st; rep from * to end of round. (18 sts)
Rounds 3–11: 1sc in each st.
Stuff lightly.
Round 12: *1sc into next st, sc2tog; rep from * to end of round. (12 sts)
Round 13: Sc2tog until opening is closed.
Fasten off.

LEGS (make 2)

Using A, 2ch, 6sc in second ch from hook.
Round 1: *1sc in next st, 2sc in next st; rep from * to end of round. (9 sts)
Rounds 2–4: 1sc in each st.
Round 5: Sc2tog, 1sc in each st to end of round. (8 sts)
Rounds 6–12: 1sc in each st.
Fasten off.

ARMS (make 2)

Using B, make 2ch, 5sc in second ch from hook.
Round 1: *1sc in next st, 2sc in next st; rep from * once, 1sc in last st. (7 sts)
Rounds 2–9: 1sc in each st.
Fasten off.

MAKING UP

Pin and sew body to head. Do not stuff legs, pin and sew to body. Stuff arms, pin and sew to body. Embroider mouth, eyebrows, and eyelashes. Tie ribbon or scarf around the neck and stitch in place.

HAIR

Using C, cut approx 50 strands each around 12in (32cm). Fold each strand in half and loop through each stitch around the crown of the doll's head. Cut more strands if necessary. Gather up hair and style into a bun at the top. Stitch in place.

DRESS

Using B, make 24ch, ss in first ch to form a ring.
Rounds 1–4: 1sc in each st. (24 sts)
Round 5: Sc2tog, 1sc in each of next 11 sts, sc2tog, 1sc in each st to end of round. (22 sts)
Round 6: Sc2tog, 1sc in each of next 10 sts, sc2tog, 1sc in each st to end of round. (20 sts)
Round 7: 1sc in each st.
Round 8: Sc2tog, 1sc in next 9 sts, sc2tog, 1sc in each st to end of round. (18 sts)
Round 9: Sc2tog, 1sc in next 8 sts, sc2tog, 1sc in each st to last st, ss to first st. (16 sts)
Fasten off.

Bottom of dress:
Turn dress upside down, join yarn at start of round.
Round 1: 2sc in first st, 1sc in each of next 11 sts, 2sc in next st, 1sc in each st to end of round. (26 sts)
Round 2: 2sc in first st, 1sc in each of next 12 sts, 2sc in next st, 1sc in each st to end of round. (28 sts)
Rounds 3–6: 1sc in each st, ending last round ss in first st.
Fasten off.

Left shoulder:
Turn dress right way up and work shoulders. With fasten-off point on your right, join yarn in third st in towards center.
Row 1: 1sc in each of next 3 sts, turn. (3 sts)
Row 2: 1sc in each of next 2 sts, turn. (2 sts)
Row 3: Sc2tog, turn. (1 st)
Row 4: 1sc in st, turn.
Row 5: 2sc in st, turn. (2 sts)
Row 6: 1sc in each of next 2 sts, turn. (2 sts)
Row 7: 2sc in next st, 1sc in next st. (3 sts)
Fasten off.

Right shoulder:
Leave 2 sts free after left shoulder, join yarn to next st and work as left shoulder.
Try dress on doll, pin and sew straps in place to back of dress.

MUMMY

Mummy has had all her brains sucked out through her nose and mouth and has then been stuffed with straw and covered in bandages. When she talks she makes Ancient Egyptian and Ptolemaic Greek sound rather like, "Mmmph, mmph, urgrrr..."

MATERIALS

Pure wool light worsted (DK) yarn:
Head, Body, Legs, Arms: ½ × 1¾oz (50g) ball—approx 57.5yd (52.5m)—of off-white
Safety eyes
Fiberfill stuffing
Two lengths of crêpe bandage, each 1 × 82in (2.5 × 208cm)
Crochet hook size: F/5 (4mm)

ABBREVIATIONS

Ch chain
Rep repeat
Sc single crochet
Sc2tog *insert hook into next st and draw up a loop; rep from * once, yarn over, draw through all 3 loops on hook.
Ss slip stitch
St(s) stitch(es)

SIZE

Approx height: 8in (21cm)

HEAD

Make 2ch, 6sc in second ch from hook.
Round 1: 2sc in each st. (12 sts)
Round 2: *1sc in next st, 2sc in next st; rep from * to end of round. (18 sts)
Round 3: *1sc in each of next 2 sts, 2sc in next st; rep from * to end of round. (24 sts)
Rounds 4–6: 1sc in each st.
Round 7: *1sc in each of next 2 sts, sc2tog; rep from * to end of round. (18 sts)
Round 8: *1sc in next st, sc2tog; rep from * to end of round. (12 sts)
Insert safety eyes and then stuff head.
Round 9: Sc2tog until opening is closed.
Fasten off.

BODY

Make 2ch, 6sc in second ch from hook.
Round 1: 2sc in each st. (12 sts)
Round 2: *1sc in next st, 2sc in next st; rep from * to end of round. (18 sts)
Rounds 3–11: 1sc in each st.
Stuff body lightly.
Round 12: *1sc in next st, sc2tog; rep from * to end of round. (12 sts)
Round 13: Sc2tog until opening is closed.
Fasten off.

LEGS (make 2)

Make 2ch, 5sc in second ch from hook.
Round 1: *1sc in next st, 2sc in next st; rep from * once, 1sc in last st. (7 sts)
Rounds 2–9: 1sc in each st.
Fasten off.

ARMS (make 2)

Make 2ch, 6sc in second ch from hook.
Round 1: *1sc in next st, 2sc in next st; rep from * to end of round. (9 sts)
Rounds 2–10: 1sc in each st.
Fasten off.

MAKING UP

Pin and sew body to head. Stuff legs and arms and attach to body.

Starting at head, wrap one of the bandages downwards leaving a space for eyes. Continue to wrap around arms, body, and legs, adding second bandage when necessary.

MR ALIEN

Mr Alien, or Geoffrey to his friends, is on another planet. He goes circuit training at weekends but has difficulties with the cross trainer because he has three feet. He loves listening to John Cooper Clarke, a punk poet from Manchester, England.

MATERIALS

Pure wool light worsted (DK) yarn:
Body, Head, Arms: ½ × 1¾oz (50g) ball—approx 62yd (56.5m)—of pale green (A)
Ears: Scraps of cream (B)
Hat: ¼ × 1¾oz (50g) ball—approx 31yd (28.5m)—of black (C)
Shoes: Scraps of orange, turquoise and red (D)
Orange safety eyes
Fiberfill stuffing
Mouth: Small piece black felt
Tongue: Small piece red felt
Crochet hook size: F/5 (4mm)

ABBREVIATIONS

Ch chain
Rep repeat
Sc single crochet
Sc2tog *insert hook into next st and draw up a loop; rep from * once, yarn over, draw through all 3 loops on hook.
Ss slip stitch
St(s) stitch(es)

SIZE

Approx height: 7in (18cm)

BODY & HEAD

Using A, make 2ch, 6sc in second ch from hook.
Round 1: 2sc in each st. (12 sts)
Round 2: *1sc in next st, 2sc in next st; rep from * to end of round. (18 sts)
Round 3: *1sc in each of next 2 sts, 2sc in next st; rep from * to end of round. (24 sts)
Round 4: *1sc in each of next 3 sts, 2sc in next st; rep from * to end of round. (30 sts)
Rounds 5–16: 1sc in each st.
Round 17: 1sc in each of first 12 sts, 2sc in each of next 6 sts, 1sc in last 12 sts. (36 sts)
Rounds 18–25: 1sc in each st.
Round 26: *1sc in each of next 4 sts, sc2tog; rep from * to end of round. (30 sts)
Round 27: *1sc in each of next 3 sts, sc2tog; rep from * to end of round. (24 sts)
Round 28: *1sc in each of next 2 sts, sc2tog; rep from * to end of round. (18 sts)
Round 29: *1sc in next st, sc2tog; rep from * to end of round. (12 sts)
Insert safety eyes and then stuff.
Round 30: Sc2tog until opening is closed.
Fasten off.

ARMS (make 2)

Using A, make 2ch, 6sc in second ch from hook.
Round 1: 2sc in each st. (12 sts)
Round 2: *1sc in each of next 2 sts, 2sc in next st; rep from * to end of round. (16 sts)
Rounds 3–4: 1sc in each st.
Round 5: *1sc in each of next 2 sts, sc2tog; rep from * to end of round. (12 sts)
Rounds 6–12: 1sc in each st.
Fasten off.

EARS (make 2)

Using B, make 2ch, 4sc in second ch from hook.
Rounds 1–3: 1sc in each st. (4 sts)
Round 4: [1sc in next st, 2sc in next st] twice. (6 sts)
Round 5: 2sc in each st. (12 sts)
Ss in next st. Fasten off.

TOP HAT

Using C, make 2ch, 6sc in second ch from hook.
Round 1: 2sc in each st. (12 sts)
Round 2: 2sc in each st. (24 sts)
Round 3: Working in back loops only, 1sc in each st. (24 sts)
Round 4: *1sc in each of next 2 sts, sc2tog; rep from * to end of round. (18 sts)
Rounds 5–6: 1sc in each st. (18 sts)
Round 7: Working in front loops only, *1sc in next st, 2sc in next st; rep from * to end of round. (27 sts)
Round 8: *1sc in each of next 2 sts, 2sc in next st; rep from * to end of round. (36 sts)
Fasten off.

SHOES (make 3, in different colors)

Using D, make 6ch.

Round 1: 2sc in second ch from hook. 1sc in each of next 3ch, 3sc in last ch. Working on other side of chain, 1sc in each of next 3ch, 2sc in last ch. (14 sts)

Round 2: 1sc in each st. (14 sts)

Round 3: 1sc in each of next 4 sts, sc2tog twice, 1sc in each of last 6 sts. (12 sts)

Round 4: 1sc in each of next 3 sts, sc2tog, 1sc, sc2tog, 1sc in each of last 4 sts. (10 sts)

Fasten off.

MAKING UP

Stuff arms lightly, pin and sew to body. Flatten out shoes from top and sew onto body. Pin and sew ears onto side of head. Turn hat right side out and attach hat to top of head. Sew in any ends.

MOUTH

Using templates on page 108, cut out mouth with teeth from black felt and tongue shape from red felt. Pin and sew mouth and tongue in place.

MRS ALIEN

Mrs Alien is somewhat bigger than Mr Alien. She doesn't like cats or having her photo taken, although the children do; they are called Lucy, Guy, and Alyce. She recently bought a 3D TV but couldn't get the glasses to fit because her eyes are too high on her head.

MATERIALS

Pure wool light worsted (DK) yarn:
Body, Head, Legs, Babies: 2 × 1¾oz (50g) balls—approx 248yd (225m)—of pale green (A)
Eye surround, Teeth: Scraps of white (B)
Eye pupil: Scrap of black (C)
Antenna: Scrap of purple (D)
Lips: ⅛ × 1¾oz (50g) ball—approx 27.5yd (25m)—of red (E)
Fiberfill stuffing
Pouch: Small piece of lightweight purple cotton fabric
Crochet hook size: E/4 (3.5mm)

ABBREVIATIONS

Ch chain
Rep repeat
Sc single crochet
Sc2tog *insert hook into next st and draw up a loop; rep from * once, yarn over, draw through all 3 loops on hook.
Ss slip stitch
St(s) stitch(es)

SIZE

Approx height: 12in (30cm)

BODY

Using A, make 4ch, ss in first ch to form a ring.
Round 1: 8sc in ring. Place st marker into loop on hook.
Round 2: 2sc in each st. (16 sts)
Round 3: *2sc in next st, 1sc in next st; rep to end of round. (24 sts)
Round 4: *2sc in next st, 1sc in each of next 2 sts; rep from * to end of round. (32 sts)
Round 5: *2sc in next st, 1sc in each of next 3 sts; rep from * to end of round. (40 sts)
Round 6: *2sc in next st, 1sc in each of next 4 sts; rep from * to end of round. (48 sts)
Round 7: *2sc in next st, 1sc in each of next 5 sts; rep from * to end of round. (56 sts)
Round 8: *2sc in next st, 1sc in each of next 6 sts; rep from * to end of round. (64 sts)
Rounds 9–18: 1sc in each st. (64 sts)
Round 19: 1sc in each of next 24 sts, 16ch, skip next 16 sts, 1sc in each st to end of round. (64 sts)
Round 20: 1sc in each of next 24 sts, 16sc in 16 ch from previous round, 1sc in each of next 24 sts. (64 sts)
Round 21: *Sc2tog, 1sc in each of next 6 sts; rep from * to end of round. (56 sts)
Rounds 22–23: 1sc in each st. (56 sts)
Round 24: *Sc2tog, 1sc in each of next 5sts; rep from * to end of round. (48 sts)
Rounds 25–26: 1sc in each st. (48 sts)
Round 27: *Sc2tog, 1sc in each of next 4 sts; rep from * to end of round. (40 sts)
Rounds 28–29: 1sc in each st. (40 sts)
Round 30: *Sc2tog, 1sc in each of next 3 sts; rep from * to end of round. (32 sts)
Rounds 31–32: 1sc in each st. (32 sts)
Stuff body.
Round 33: *Sc2tog, 1sc in each of next 2 sts; rep from * to end of round. (24 sts)
Rounds 34–35: 1sc in each st. (24 sts)
Fasten off.

HEAD

Using A, make 4ch, ss in first ch to form a ring.
Round 1: 6sc in ring. Place st marker into loop on hook.
Round 2: *2sc in next st, 1sc in next st; rep from * to end of round. (9 sts)
Round 3: 2sc in each st. (18 sts)
Round 4: 1sc in each st. (18 sts)
Round 5: *2sc in next st, 1sc in next st; rep from * to end of round. (27 sts)
Round 6: 1sc in each st. (27 sts)
Round 7: *2sc in next st, 1sc in each of next 2 sts; rep from * to end of round. (36 sts)
Round 8: 1sc in each st. (36 sts)
Round 9: Rep Round 7. (48 sts)
Rounds 10–12: 1sc in each st. (48 sts)
Round 13: *2sc in next st, 1sc in each of next 3 sts; rep from * to end of round. (60 sts)
Round 14: 1sc in each st. (60 sts)
Round 15: *Sc2tog, 1sc in each of next 3 sts; rep from * to end of round. (48 sts)
Round 16: 1sc in each st. (48 sts)
Round 17: *Sc2tog, 1sc in each of next 2 sts; rep from * to end of round. (36 sts)
Round 18: 1sc in each st. (36 sts)
Round 19: *Sc2tog, 1sc in next st; rep from * to end of round. (24 sts)
Round 20: 1sc in each st. (24 sts)
Stuff head.
Round 21: Sc2tog around. (12 sts)
Round 22: Rep Round 21. (6 sts)
Fasten off.

LEGS (make 3)

Using A, make 4ch, ss in first ch to form a ring.

Round 1: 6sc in ring. Place st marker into loop on hook.

Round 2: *2sc in next st, 1sc in next st; rep from * to end of round. (9 sts)

Round 3: 1sc in each st. (9 sts)

Round 4: 2sc in each st. (18 sts)

Round 5: 1sc in each st. (18 sts)

Round 6: *2sc in next st, 1sc in next st; rep from * to end of round. (27 sts)

Rounds 7–8: 1sc in each st. (27 sts)

Fasten off.

EYES (make 2)

Surround:

Using B, make 4ch, ss in first ch to form a ring.

Round 1: 6sc in ring. Place st marker into loop on hook.

Round 2: 1sc in each st. (6 sts)

Round 3: 2sc in each st. (12 sts)

Round 4: Sc2tog around. (6 sts)

Round 5: Sc2tog around. (3 sts)

Fasten off.

Pupil:

Using C, make 4ch, ss in first ch to form a ring. Work 4sc in ring, ss in first sc.

Fasten off.

ANTENNA

Using D double throughout and leaving a long end of yarn at beginning and end, make 20ch.

Fasten off.

MAKING UP

Pin and sew head to body. Stuff legs, pin and sew to body, with two legs at the back and one in front. Sew pupil to center of eye surround using photo as guide. Pin and sew eyes to top of head. Tie ends of antenna together (one end can be used to attach antenna to head). Twist the chain several times and stitch lightly to hold in twisted shape. Stitch antenna to head.

LIPS & TEETH

Top lip:

The mouth is approx 3½in (9cm) wide. Use photo on page 23 as a guide. Using E, start at one end and sew a row of closely packed vertical lines over a single crochet row to end. If necessary, work twice for extra thickness.

Tip: Follow the rows of single crochet to embroider the top lip—each part of the lip is stitched over one row of single crochet.

Bottom lip & teeth:

Make alternating red and white triangles for teeth, as follows.

Using B or E, embroider a row of triangles the length of mouth and across the row of single crochet immediately below top lip. Bring needle up through bottom point of each triangle and, working towards the top, fill in gap of triangle with stitches.

Repeat as necessary.

BABY POUCH

Step 1: Cut two semicircles of fabric with the straight edge to match opening in body.

Step 2: With RS together, stitch together along curved edge, leaving straight edge open.

Step 3: Turn over straight edge of pouch and press.

Step 4: Insert pouch into opening and sew folded edges neatly to opening edges, creating baby pouch.

Step 5: Stuff body below pouch, checking that pouch lies flat, then stuff above pouch, ensuring stuffing is sufficiently loose to allow room for baby aliens.

BABY ALIEN

BODY (make 3 or 4)

Using A, make 4ch, ss in first ch to form a ring.

Round 1: 6sc in ring. Place st mark into loop on hook.

Round 2: 2sc in each st. (12 sts)

Round 3: 1sc in each st. (12 sts)

Round 4: *2sc in next st, 1sc in next st; rep from * to end of round. (18 sts)

Round 5: Sc2tog to end of round. (9 sts)

Round 6: Sc2 tog, 1sc in next st; rep from * to end of round. (6 sts)

Round 7: Sc2tog around. (3 sts)

Fasten off.

HEAD (make 3 or 4)

Using A, make 4ch, ss in first ch to form a ring.

Round 1: 6sc in ring. Place st marker in loop on hook.

Round 2: *2sc in next st, 1sc in next st; rep from * to end of round. (9 sts)

Round 3: 1sc in each st. (9 sts)

Round 4: *Sc2tog, 1sc in next st: rep from * to end of round. (6 sts)

Round 5: Sc2tog around. (3 sts)

Fasten off.

Do not stuff.

EYES (make 2 for each head)

Surround:

Using B, make 4ch, ss in first ch to form a ring. Fasten off, leaving long ends of yarn for sewing in.

Pupil:

Using C, make a running stitch between chain stitches then darn between black stitches to create black center, using the photo below as a guide.

ANTENNA

Using purple yarn, make 6ch, skip first ch, ss in each ch to end.

Fasten off.

MAKING UP

Stuff body lightly and sew to head. Pin and sew eyes and antenna to head. Embroider mouth.

CHAPTER 2
FAMOUS SCARIES

The Famous Scaries are having a get together. Severus
will be gnawing his sailor's leg—it's his favorite canapé.
Dom will be sipping anemic blood red cocktails, his new
take on a martini, and ignoring the Headless Horseman
and Redeye's attempts to impress the ladies. The
Invisible Man will be having a good old gossip
with Bernard Bigfoot about Walter the Werewolf's
latest exploits.

SEVERUS THE SHARK

Severus's teeth are a little wobbly and they are shiny white and as sharp as knives. When he feels hungry he roams the seas looking for missing sailors. He has eaten a whole boatful of men before, but he doesn't like women or children because they taste too sweet.

MATERIALS

Pure wool light worsted (DK) yarn:
Head, Body, Fins, Tail: ½ × 1¾oz (50g) ball
—approx 60yd (55m)—of gray (A)
Mouth, Underside: ¼ × 1¾oz (50g) ball
—approx 31yd (28.5m)—of white (B)
Leg: ⅙ × 1¾oz (50g) ball—approx 14yd
(12.5m)—of beige (C)
Tongue, Blood: Scrap of red (D)
Safety eyes
Fiberfill stuffing
Teeth: Approx 15 tooth-shaped beads
Crochet hook size: E/4 (3.5mm)

ABBREVIATIONS

Ch chain
Cont continue
Rep repeat
Sc single crochet
Sc2tog *insert hook into next st and draw
up a loop; rep from * once, yarn over,
draw through all 3 loops on hook.
Sc3tog *insert hook into next st and draw
up a loop; rep from * twice, yarn over,
draw through all 4 loops on hook.
Ss slip stitch
St(s) stitch(es)

SIZE

Approx length: 8¼in (21cm)

TIP

When stuffing the shark, do not over stuff
so that the stitches show through.

HEAD & BODY

Using A, make 2ch, 6sc in second ch from hook.
Round 1: *1sc in next st, 2sc in next st; rep
from * to end of round. (9 sts)
Round 2: *2sc in each of next 2 sts, 1sc in each
st to last 2 sts, 2sc in each st. (13 sts)
Round 3: Rep Round 2. (17 sts)
Round 4: 1sc in each st. (17 sts)
Round 5: 1sc in each of next 4 sts, 2sc in each
of next 2 sts, 1sc in each of next 5 sts, 2sc in
each of next 2 sts, 1sc in each of last 4 sts.
(21 sts)
Round 6: 1sc in each of next 10 sts, 2sc in each
of next 2 sts, 1sc in each of last 9 sts. (23 sts)
Round 7: 1sc in each st. (23 sts)
Round 8: 1sc in each of next 4 sts, 2sc in each
of next 2 sts, 1sc in each of next 11 sts, 2sc
in each of next 2 sts, 1sc in each of last
4 sts. (27 sts)
Rounds 9–18: 1sc in each st. (27 sts)
Round 19: *1sc in each of next 7 sts, sc2tog;
rep from * to end of round. (24 sts)
Rounds 20–24: 1sc in each st. (24 sts)
Round 25: *1sc in each of next 4 sts, sc2tog;
rep from * to end of round. (20 sts)
Insert safety eyes and stuff head.

Rounds 26–29: 1sc in each st. (20 sts)
Round 30: *1sc in each of next 3 sts, sc2tog;
rep from * to end of round. (16 sts)
Round 31: 1sc in each st. (16 sts)
Round 32: *1sc in each of next 2 sts, sc2tog;
rep from * to end of round. (12 sts)
Add more stuffing.
Round 33: 1sc in each st. (12 sts)
Round 34: *1sc in next st, sc2tog; rep from
* to end of round. (8 sts)
Add a little more stuffing if necessary.
Do not fasten off.
The end of the shark is closed so that it is flat
and not round. Gently squeeze the sts
together so there is a short flat seam and
sc the sts together. (4 sts).
Fasten off, leaving a long tail.

MOUTH

Using B, make 2ch, 6sc in second ch from hook.
Round 1: 2sc in each of next 5 sts, turn. (10 sts)
Working in rows from here on:
Row 1: 1ch, in back loops only make 1sc in
each st to end, do not turn. (10 sts).
Make 1ch, 1sc in same st, 1sc in each st across
the bottom.

UNDERSIDE

Row 1: 1sc in each st, turn. (5 sts)

Row 2: 2sc in first st, 1sc in each of next 3 sts, 2sc in last st, turn. (7 sts)

Row 3: 2sc in first st, 1sc in each of next 5 sts, 2sc in last st, turn. (9 sts)

Rows 4–14: 1sc in each st, turn. (9 sts)

Row 15: Sc2tog in first st, 1sc in each st to last 2 sts, sc2tog, turn. (7 sts)

Row 16–17: Rep Row 15. (3 sts)

Row 18: 1sc in each st, turn. (3 sts)

Row 19: Sc3tog.

Fasten off, leaving a long tail.

TONGUE

Using D, make 6ch, 2sc in second ch from hook. 1sc in each of next 3 ch, 3sc in last ch. Working on other side of chain, 1sc in each of next 3 ch, 2sc in last ch, join with ss into first sc.

Fasten off.

DORSAL FIN (top fin)

Using A, 2ch, 4sc in second ch from hook.

Round 1: 2sc in first st, 1sc in each st to end of round. (5 sts)

Round 2: 2sc in first st, 1sc in each of next 2 sts, 2sc in next st, 1sc in last st. (7 sts)

Round 3: 2sc in first st, 1sc in each of next 2 sts, 2sc in next st, 1sc in each of last 3 sts. (9 sts)

Round 4: 2sc in first st, 1sc in each of next 3 sts, 2sc in next st, 1sc in each of last 4 sts. (11 sts)

Round 5: 2sc in first st, 1sc in each of next 5 sts, 2sc in next st, 1sc in each of last 4 sts. (13 sts)

Round 6: 2sc in first st, 1sc in each of next 6 sts, 2sc in next st, 1sc in each of last 5 sts. (15 sts)

Fasten off leaving a long tail.

SIDE FINS (make 2)

Using A, 2ch, 4sc in second ch from hook.

Round 1: 2sc in first st, 1sc in each st to end of round. (5 sts)

Round 2: 2sc in first st, 1sc in each of next 2 sts, 2sc in next st, 1sc in last st. (7 sts)

Round 3: 2sc in first st, 1sc in each of next 2 sts, 2sc in next st, 1sc in each of last 3 sts. (9 sts)

Round 4: 2sc in first st, 1sc in each of next 3 sts, 2sc in next st, 1sc in each of last 4 sts. (11 sts)

Round 5: 2sc in first st, 1sc in each of next 5 sts, 2sc in next st, 1sc in each of last 4 sts. (13 sts)

Fasten off.

TAIL FIN

Using A, 2ch, 4sc in second ch from hook.

Round 1: 2sc in first st, 1sc in each of next 3 sts. (5 sts)

Round 2: 2sc in first st, 1sc in each of next 4 sts. (6 sts)

Round 3: 2sc in first st, 1sc in each of next 5 sts. (7 sts)

Round 4: 1sc in each st. (7 sts)

Round 5: 1sc in each of next 3 sts, sc2tog, 1sc in each of next 2 sts, 2sc in last st. (7 sts)

Rounds 6–7: Rep Round 5. (7 sts)

Round 8: 1sc in each st. (7 sts)

Round 9: 1sc in each of next 3 sts, sc2tog, 1sc in each of last 2 sts. (6 sts)

Round 10: 1sc in each of next 2 sts, sc2tog, 1sc in each of last 2 sts. (5 sts)

Fasten off leaving a long tail.

SEVERED LEG

Using C, make 6ch, 2sc in second ch from hook.

Round 1: 1sc in each of next 3 ch, 3sc in last ch. Working on other side of chain, 1sc in each of next 3ch, 2sc in last ch. (14 sts)

Cont working in back of loops only.

Round 2: 1sc in each st. (14 sts)

Round 3: 1sc in next 4 sts, sc2tog twice, 1sc in each of last 6 sts. (12 sts)

Round 4: 1sc in next 3 sts, sc2tog, 1sc, sc2tog, 1sc in each of last 4 sts. (10 sts)

Round 5: 1sc in next 2 sts, sc2tog, 1sc, sc2tog, 1sc in each of last 3 sts. (8 sts)

Cont working in both loops.

Round 6: 1sc in each st. (8 sts)

Cont working 1sc in each st until leg measures approx 2in (5cm).

Fasten off.

MAKING UP

Place tongue in position inside mouth so that bottom lip is curling upwards. Sew in position. Pin and sew underside underneath body, leaving mouth open. Using A, make a running stitch along outside edge of nose area to flatten and give a shark-like appearance. Sew in bead teeth. Make a running stitch along outside edge of sides of dorsal fin, leaving bottom open for sewing onto body. Pin and sew dorsal fin in position on top of body. Pin and sew side fins in position, one on each side of body.

Tighten up hole at end of tail by weaving in and out of stitches. Sew in end. Flatten out tail, neaten ends. Place a pin marker across top of back and line up tail in position. Pin it carefully before sewing on—longer part of tail points downward.

Stuff severed leg. Sew opening so it remains flat, do not tighten to a point when sewing in end. Thread a tapestry needle with D and embroider across top of leg. *using D, join yarn into top of severed leg and make 8ch, ss into fourth ch from hook, ss into next ch and fasten off. Rep from * 3 times more.

Fasten off.

Sew leg inside shark's mouth.

DOMINIC THE VAMPIRE

It's true that Dom is personally responsible for the bloody deaths of some 200 young people in the Brooklyn area. It is also true that he keeps a set of size G/6 crochet hooks hidden beneath his cloak and uses them to puncture the necks of his victims.

MATERIALS

Pure wool light worsted (DK) yarn:

Shoes, Body, Arms, Hair: ½ × 1¾oz (50g) ball—approx 62yd (56.5m)—of black (A)

Legs, Mouth: ¼ × 1¾oz (50g) ball—approx 31yd (28.5m)—of gray (B)

Head: ¼ × 1¾oz (50g) ball—approx 31yd (28.5m)—of white (C)

Eye surround, Fangs: Piece of red felt

Safety eyes

Fiberfill stuffing

Cloak: 18 × 9in (46 × 23cm) silver/black fabric (allow more if hemming is necessary)

Crochet hook size: E/4 (3.5mm)

ABBREVIATIONS

Beg beginning

Ch chain

Cont continue

Rep repeat

Sc single crochet

Sc2tog *insert hook into next st and draw up a loop; rep from * once, yarn over, draw through all 3 loops on hook.

Ss slip stitch

St(s) stitch(es)

SIZE

Approx height: 8½in (22cm)

SHOES, LEGS, BODY & HEAD

Right shoe:

Using A, make 6ch.

Round 1: 2sc in second ch from hook. 1sc in each of next 3ch, 3sc in last ch. Working on other side of chain, 1sc in each of next 3ch, 2sc in last ch. (14 sts)

Cont working in back of loops only.

Round 2: 1sc in each st. (14 sts)

Round 3: 1sc in next 4 sts, sc2tog twice, 1sc in each of last 6 sts. (12 sts)

Round 4: 1sc in next 3 sts, sc2tog, 1sc, sc2tog, 1sc in each of last 4 sts. (10 sts)

Right leg:

Change to B, begin working in both loops.

Round 5: 1sc in next 2 sts, sc2tog, 1sc, sc2tog, 1sc in each of last 3 sts. (8 sts)

Rounds 6–10: 1sc in each st. (8 sts)

Round 11: [1sc in each of next 2 sts, 2sc in next st] twice, 1sc in each of last 2 sts. (10 sts)

Rounds 12–17: 1sc in each st.

Fasten off.

Left shoe & leg:

Rep first shoe and leg. Do not fasten off before stuffing.

Stuff legs and pin together with long quilting pins, so that both feet are facing in the same direction.

Body:

Insert hook into unfastened-off st on second leg. Mark beg of round into first st with a st marker.

Round 1: 1sc in each of next 5 sts around leg towards back. Insert hook into corresponding st of other leg. Join legs together by making 1sc in each of next 10 sts of first leg, make 1sc into each of next 5 sts of second leg. (20 sts)

Rounds 2–3: 1sc in each st. (20 sts)

Change to A.

Rounds 4–13: 1sc in each st. (20 sts)

Round 14: *1sc in next st, sc2tog; rep from * to last 2 sts, 1sc in each st. (14 sts)

Round 15: Rep Round 14. (10 sts)

Stuff body. Do not fasten off.

Head:

Change to C.

Round 1: 1sc in each st. (10 sts)

Round 2: *1sc in next st, 2sc in next st; rep from * to end of round. (15 sts)

Round 3: *1sc in each of next 2 sts, 2sc in next st; rep from * to end of round. (20 sts)

Round 4: *1sc in each of next 3 sts, 2sc in next st; rep from * to end of round. (25 sts)

Rounds 5–9: 1sc in each st. (25 sts)

Round 10: *1sc in next st, sc2tog; rep from * to end of round. (17 sts)

Cut two small circles in red felt. Cut a hole in the middle of each, insert safety eyes and push into position in face. Stuff head.

Round 11: *1sc in next st, sc2tog; rep from * to last 2 sts, sc2tog. (11 sts)

Round 12: Sc2tog around.

Fasten off.

ARMS (make 2)

Using A, make 2ch, 5sc in second ch from hook.

Round 1: *1sc in next st, 2sc in next st; rep from * once, 1sc in last st. (7 sts)

Next round: Work 1sc in each st around until arm measures 3½in (9cm).

Fasten off. Do not stuff.

MAKING UP

Hand sew felt eye surrounds onto face. Pin and sew arms to body. Using B, embroider mouth. Cut out two triangular-shaped fangs and hand sew in place at side of mouth.

HAIR

Using A threaded in tapestry needle, embroider vampire-style hair with a "V" shape at the front.

CLOAK

Make a small hem along each side if the fabric frays. Measure down approx 2in (5cm) from top for the collar, then gather around for neck. Hand sew cloak onto doll.

MATERIALS

Pure wool light worsted (DK) yarn:

Boots, Mouth, Gilet: ¼ × 1¾oz (50g) ball
—approx 31yd (28.5m)—of black (A)

Pants: ¼ × 1¾oz (50g) ball—approx 31yd
(28.5m) of blue (B)

Body, Ruffle, Arms: ¼ × 1¾oz (50g) ball
—approx 31yd (28.5m)—of cream (C)

Hands, Head: ¼ × 1¾oz (50g) ball—
approx 31yd (28.5m)—of beige (D)

Goatee, Hair: Small amount of brown (E)

Blood: Small amount of red (F)

Mustache: Small piece black felt

Safety eyes

Fiberfill stuffing

Crochet hook size: F/5 (4mm)

ABBREVIATIONS

Beg beginning

Ch chain

Dc double crochet

Rep repeat

Sc single crochet

Sc2tog *insert hook into next st and draw
up a loop; rep from * once, yarn over,
draw through all 3 loops on hook.

Ss slip stitch

St(s) stitch(es)

SIZE

Approx height: 7in (18cm)

HERMAN THE HEADLESS HORSEMAN

Herman haunts the local woodland on the edge of town. His head was chopped off in a fight with his best friend, who went off with one of his girlfriends. Despite this setback, he is very jolly and handsome, and tells a good tale—and particularly loves beautiful ladies.

BOOTS, LEGS & BODY

Right leg:

Using A, 6ch.

Round 1: 2sc in second ch from hook. 1sc in each of next 3ch, 3sc in last ch. Working on other side of chain, 1sc in each of next 3ch, 2sc in last ch. (14 sts)

Continue in A working in back of loops only.

Round 2: 1sc in each st. (14 sts)

Round 3: 1sc in each of next 4 sts, sc2tog twice, 1sc in each of last 6 sts. (12 sts)

Round 4: 1sc in each of next 3 sts, sc2tog, 1sc, sc2tog, 1sc in each of last 4 sts. (10 sts)

Round 5: 1sc in each of next 2 sts, sc2tog, 1sc, sc2tog, 1sc in each of last 3 sts. (8 sts)

Work in both loops.

Rounds 6–9: 1sc in each st. (8 sts)

Change to B, begin working in back loops only.

Round 10: 1sc in each st. (8 sts)

Round 11: [1sc in each of next 2 sts, 2sc in next st] twice, 1sc in each of last 2 sts. (10 sts)

Work in both loops.

Rounds 12–17: 1sc in each st.

Fasten off.

Boot cuff:

Reattach A at back of boot into front loop of Round 9 (top of boot).

3ch, *make 2dc in each front loop around. Ss into third of first 3-ch.

Fasten off, sew in ends.

Left leg:

Repeat first boot and leg. Do not fasten off before stuffing.

Make boot cuff as first leg.

Stuff legs. Pin legs together with long quilting pins, so both feet are facing in same direction.

Body:

Cont in B, insert hook into unfastened-off st on second leg. Mark beg of round into first st with st marker.

Round 1: 1sc in each of 5 sts around leg towards back. Insert hook into corresponding st of other leg. Join legs together by making 1sc in each of next 10 sts of first leg, make 1sc into each of next 5 sts of second leg. (20 sts)

Rounds 2–5: 1sc in each st. (20 sts)

Change to C.

Rounds 6–13: 1sc in each st. (20 sts)

Round 14: *1sc, sc2tog; rep from * to last 2 sts, 1sc in each st. (14 sts)

Round 15: Rep Round 14. (10 sts)

Stuff body.

Round 16: Sc2tog around.

Fasten off.

SHIRT RUFFLE

Using C, make 23ch.

Round 1: Make 3dc in third ch from hook, *skip 2ch, make 3dc in next st; rep from * once more. Make 2dc in each ch to last 3-ch. Make 3dc in each of last 3-ch.

Fasten off, leaving a long tail.

HANDS & ARMS (make 2)

Using D, 2ch, 5sc in second ch from hook.

Round 1: *1sc in next st, 2sc in next st; rep from * once, 1sc in last st. (7 sts)

Rounds 2–4: 1sc in each st.

Change to C.

Rounds 5–17: 1sc in each st.

Fasten off.

GILET

Work in rows.

Using A, make 25ch, 1sc in second ch from hook.

Round 1: 1sc in each ch to end. (24 sts)

Rows 2–5: 1ch, 1sc in each st. (24 sts)

Row 6: 1ch, skip 1 st, 1sc in each st to end. (23 sts)

Row 7: Rep Row 6. (22 sts)

Row 8: Rep Row 6. (21 sts)

Row 9: Rep Row 6. (20 sts)

Right front of gilet:

Row 10: 1ch, turn, skip 1 st, 1sc in each of last 4 sts. (4 sts)

Rows 11–16: 1ch, 1sc in each st. (4 sts)

Fasten off.

Left front of gilet:

Rows 10–16: Reattach yarn on other side of gilet. Work as for Right front of gilet.

Center back of gilet:

Reattach yarn at one end in between two sides.

Row 1: Work 1sc into each of next 10 sts.

Rows 2–4: 1ch, 1sc in each st.

Row 5: 1ch, 2sc in first st, 1sc in each st to last st, 2sc in last st. (12 sts)

Row 6: Rep Row 5. (14 sts)

Row 7: Rep Row 5. (16 sts)

Fasten off, leaving a long tail.

HEAD

Using D, 2ch, 5sc in second ch from hook.

Round 1: 2sc in each st. (10 sts)

Round 2: *1sc in next st, 2sc in next st; rep from* to end of round. (15 sts)

Round 3: *1sc in each of next 2 sts, 2sc in next st; rep from * to end of round. (20 sts)

Rounds 4–7: 1sc in each st.

Round 8: *1sc in each of next 2 sts, sc2tog; rep from * to end of round. (15 sts)

Round 9: *1sc in next st, sc2tog; rep from * to end of round. (10 sts)

Insert safety eyes and stuff.

Round 10: *1sc, sc2tog; rep from * to end of round. (7 sts)

Round 11: Sc2tog around round until hole is closed.

Fasten off.

MAKING UP

Sew two short ends of shirt ruffle together. Place ruffle around the neck; pin in place, gathering in places for a ruffled effect. Stitch in place.

Pin and sew arms to body.

Fold each side of the gilet into center. Sew top shoulder seam on each side. Attach to body and stitch in place one front across the other.

Embroider mouth with A.

Embroider goatee beard with E.

Cut out mustache shape from black felt and stitch in place.

HAIR

Using E, cut approx 40 strands of yarn each around 6in (15cm) long. Place across top of and down back of head. Stitch in place using a short running stitch. Add more strands if necessary and trim.

Sew head to side of body. Sew one arm around head and other arm in a curve so that hand sits on waist.

BLOOD

Neck blood:

Join F in any st around severed neck.

Pick up and make 10sc around center, join with ss into first sc.

*Make 8ch, ss into fourth ch from hook.

Fasten off.

Sew in end right down to base of ch.

Rejoin yarn into another sc; rep from * 4 or 5 more times to make more blood droplets.

Head blood:

Join F under chin. *Make 8ch, ss into fourth ch from hook.

Fasten off.

Sew in end right down to base of ch.

Rejoin yarn into another sc; rep from * 2 or 3 more times to make more blood droplets.

REDEYE, THE HEADLESS HORSEMAN'S HORSE

Redeye, the Headless Horseman's Horse, was killed in the Middle Ages for being so stubborn. A thousand red spiders brought him back to life and he is eternally indebted to them. He is a brave steed and he and the Headless Horseman prey on both innocent young women and young fillies.

MATERIALS

Pure wool light worsted (DK) yarn:
Head, Neck, Ears, Body, Legs, Forelock, Mane, Tail:
 1½ x 1¾oz (50g) balls—approx 185yd (169m)—of black (A)
Spider: Scrap of red (B)
Lurex yarn:
Headcollar: Scrap of silver (C)
Eyes: 2 x flat-back red beads
Fiberfill stuffing
Crochet hook size: F/5 (4mm)

ABBREVIATIONS

Ch chain
Rep repeat
Sc single crochet
Sc2tog *insert hook into next st and draw up a loop; rep from * once, yarn over, draw through all 3 loops on hook.
Ss slip stitch
St(s) stitch(es)

SIZE

Approx height: 7in (18cm)
Approx length: 9in (23cm)

HEAD

Using A, make 2ch, 6sc in second ch from hook.
Round 1: 2sc in each st. (12 sts)
Rounds 2–6: 1sc in each st.
Round 7: 1sc in each of next 3 sts, 2sc in each of next 6 sts, 1sc in each of last 3 sts. (18 sts)
Round 8: 1sc in each st.
Round 9: 1sc in each of first 6 sts, 2sc in each of next 6 sts, 1sc in each of last 6 sts. (24 sts)
Rounds 10–15: 1sc in each st.
Round 16: *1sc in each of next 2 sts, sc2tog; rep from * to end of round. (18 sts)
Stuff head.
Round 17: *1sc in next st, sc2tog; rep from * to end of round. (12 sts)
Round 18: *Sc2tog; rep from * to end of round. (6 sts)
Fasten off.

NECK

Using A, make 18ch, ss in first ch to form a ring.
Round 1: 1ch, 1sc in each ch to end of round.
Rounds 2–6: 1sc in each st.
Rounds 7–8: Ss in first 9 sts, 1sc in each of last 9 sts.
Fasten off.
Stuff.

EARS (make 2)

Using A, make 4ch, 1sc in second ch from hook, 1sc in next ch, 3sc in last ch.
Work in other side of ch.
1sc in each of next 2 sts, ss in first sc.
Fasten off.

BODY

Using A, make 2ch, 6sc in second ch from hook.
Round 1: 2sc in each st. (12 sts)
Round 2: *1sc in next st, 2sc in next st; rep from * to end of round. (18 sts)
Round 3: *1sc in each of next 2 sts, 2sc in next st; rep from * to end of round. (24 sts)
Round 4: *1sc in each of next 3 sts, 2sc in next st; rep from * to end of round. (30 sts)
Rounds 5–14: 1sc in each st.
Round 15: 1sc in each of first 12 sts, 2sc in each of next 6 sts, 1sc in each of last 12 sts. (36 sts)
Rounds 16–23: 1sc in each st.
Round 24: *1sc in each of next 4 sts, sc2tog; rep from * to end of round. (30 sts)
Round 25: *1sc in each of next 3 sts, sc2tog; rep from * to end of round. (24 sts)
Round 26: *1sc in each of next 2 sts, sc2tog; rep from * to end of round. (18 sts)
Round 27: *1sc in next st, sc2tog; rep from * to end of round. (12 sts)
Stuff body.
Round 28: Sc2tog until opening is closed.
Fasten off.

LEGS (make 4)

Using A, make 2ch, 6sc in second ch from hook.
Round 1: 2sc in each st. (12 sts)
Round 2: *1sc in next st, 2sc in next st: rep from * to end of round. (18 sts)
Round 3: Working in back loops only, 1sc in each st.
Round 4: Working in both loops, 1sc in each st.
Round 5: *1sc in next st, sc2tog; rep from * to end of round. (12 sts)
Rounds 6–18: 1sc in each st.
Fasten off.

MAKING UP

Attach one end of neck to back of head with the highest point at the top. Pin and sew ears in position on top of head. Pin and sew body in place to neck with straighter side at top. Stuff legs, pin, and sew to body. Glue on eye beads.

HEADCOLLAR

*Join C underneath horse's head at join to neck.
Make 28ch, or enough ch to go round horse's head behind ears. Join with ss at start of ch.
Make 5ch toward front, approx 1½in (4cm) from tip of nose, join ch to head with ss (underneath).
Make 14ch around nose to form noseband, join with ss underneath.
Make 8ch at side of face and join to neckband just underneath ear.
Fasten off.
Rep from * on other side of face.

FORELOCK & MANE

Cut lengths of A around 11½in (30cm) long. Using a crochet hook, hook strands to form a loop and thread through to secure, two at a time, through top of head at front for forelock and down one side of neck just left of center. Do not trim—leave long. If mane isn't thick enough, make another layer underneath first along neck.
Cut one strand of B and loop it through forelock; and trim forelock to approx 2½in (7.5cm).

TAIL

Cut approx 20 lengths of A, each 10½in (26cm) long. Attach to rear end of body by using crochet hook to loop all strands through.

SPIDER MOTIF

Using B, embroider spider motif on side of horse's rear.

YOHAN THE INVISIBLE MAN

Yohan is actually very good looking. He models and often spends half the day deciding what to wear. The trouble is, when he takes his bandages off he can't see himself. He believes a regular moisturizing regime is crucial.

MATERIALS

Pure wool light worsted (DK) yarn:
Pants, Jacket: ¼ × 1¾oz (50g) ball
—approx 31yd (28.5m)—of gray (A)
Shirt, Sleeves, Head: ¼ × 1¾oz (50g) ball
—approx 31yd (28.5m)—of cream (B)
Tie: Small amount of blue (C)
Shoes: Small amount of brown (D)
Bowler hat, Buttons: Small amount of
  black (E)
Wig: Small amount of brown fiberfill
Fiberfill stuffing
Length of narrow crepe bandage
Floristry wire
Brown floristry tape
Crochet hook size: F/5 (4mm)

ABBREVIATIONS

Beg beginning
Ch chain
Cont continue
Dc double
Rep repeat
Sc single crochet
Sc2tog *insert hook into next st and draw
  up a loop; rep from * once, yarn over,
  draw through all 3 loops on hook.
Ss slip stitch
St(s) stitch(es)

SIZE

Approx height: 9in (23cm)

PANTS & SHIRT

First pants leg:
Using A, make 2ch, 6sc in second ch from hook.
Round 1: 2sc in each st. (12 sts)
Rounds 2–7: 1sc in each st. (12 sts)
Round 8: Sc2tog, 1sc in each st to last 2 sts, sc2tog. (10 sts)
Rounds 9–17: 1sc in each st. (10 sts)
Fasten off.

Second pants leg:
Rep Rounds 1–17 of first leg. Do not fasten off.

Shirt:
Using B, insert hook into unfastened off st on second leg. Mark beg of round into first st with st marker.
Round 1: Keep loop at back of leg, insert hook in corresponding place on other leg and make 1sc in each st around first leg. Join at front and cont round. (20 sts)
Rounds 2–13: 1sc in each st. (20 sts)
Round 14: *1sc, sc2tog; rep from * to last 2 sts, 1sc in each st. (14 sts)
Round 15: Rep Round 14. (10 sts)
Stuff shirt.
Thread tapestry needle with end and weave around opening, pull end to close hole.

Shirt Collar:
Insert hook into neck area at front and re-join B. Make 2ch.
1dc in each st around neckline, leaving a small gap at front. Ss into same st as last dc to finish.
Fasten off.

Tie:
Join C into gap in collar. Make 4ch, ss into joining st.
Make 1sc in each st down front of shirt and 1sc over pants top.
Fasten off.

SLEEVES (make 2)

Using B, make 2ch, 6sc in second ch from hook.
Round 1: *1sc in next st, 2sc in next st; rep from * to end of round. (9 sts)
Next round: 1sc in each st until arm measures 3½in (9cm).
Fasten off.

HEAD

Using B, make 2ch, 5sc in second ch from hook.
Round 1: *2sc in each st. (10 sts)
Round 2: *1sc in next st, 2sc in next st; rep from * to end of round. (15 sts)
Round 3: *1sc in each of next 2 sts, 2sc in next st; rep from * to end of round. (20 sts)
Round 4: *1sc in each of next 3 sts, 2sc in next st; rep from * to end of round. (25 sts)
Rounds 5–8: 1sc in each st. (25 sts)
Round 9: *1sc in next st, sc2tog; rep from * to last st, 1sc. (17 sts)
Stuff head.
Round 10: *1sc in next st, sc2tog; rep from * to last 2 sts, sc2tog. (11 sts)
Round 11: Sc2tog around.
Fasten off.

MAKING UP

Sew in ends. Stuff sleeves. Take yarn end from cuff end, sew in end to center of opening and take end up through the center, so inside is hidden. Pin and sew sleeves to shirt.

Wrap head in bandages. Sew bandages to secure to head. Sew head to shirt, making sure head sits inside collar.

Wrap a length of floristry wire with brown floristry tape. Bend wire into pair of glasses and place on Yohan's face.

SHOES (make 2)

Using D, make 2ch.

Round 1: 6sc in second ch from hook. 1sc in each of next 3ch, 3sc in last ch. Working on other side of chain, 1sc in each of next 3ch, 2sc in last ch. (14 sts)

Insert st marker onto loop on hook, cont working in back of loops only.

Round 2: 1sc in each st. (14 sts)

Round 3: 1sc in next 4 sts, sc2tog twice, 1sc in each of last 6 sts. (12 sts)

Round 4: 1sc in next 3 sts, sc2tog, 1sc, sc2tog, 1sc in each of last 4 sts. (10 sts)

Stuff toes of shoes with brown stuffing. Thread through strands of black yarn or embroidery floss as laces and tie in a bow.

BOWLER HAT

Using E, make 2ch, 6sc in second ch from hook.

Round 1: 2sc in each st. (12 sts)

Round 2: *1sc in next st, 2sc in next st; rep from * to end of round. (18 sts)

Rounds 3–5: 1sc in each st.

Round 6: 2sc in each st. (36 sts)

Round 7: Sc2tog around. (18 sts)

Round 8: *1sc in next, 2sc in next st; rep from * to end of round. (27 sts)

Round 9: *1sc in each of next 2 sts, 2sc in next st; rep from * to end of round. (36 sts)

Turn inside out, sew in ends.

Form hat into bowler hat shape and add some brown fiberfill inside as hair.

JACKET

Using A, make 25ch.

Round 1: 1sc in second ch from hook, 1sc in each st to end of round. (24 sts)

Rounds 2–10: 1ch, 1sc in each st.

Do not fasten off.

Right front:

Row 11: 1ch, skip first st, 1sc in each of next 7 sts, turn. (7 sts)

Cont working on these 7 sts only.

Rows 12–17: 1ch, 1sc in each st. (7 sts)

Fasten off.

Left front:

Working on other side of jacket, rejoin yarn into first st.

Rep Rows 11–17.

Center back:

Rejoin yarn in between two sides at one end.

Row 1: 2sc in first st, 1sc from one side to other to last st, 2sc in last st. (11 sts)

Rows 2–4: 1sc in each st.

Row 5: 2sc in first st, 1sc in each st to last st, 2sc in last st. (13 sts)

Row 6: Rep Row 5. (15 sts)

Row 7: Rep Row 5. (17 sts)

Fasten off.

Sleeves:

Join yarn to top of sleeve edge.

Make 12sc around armhole edge, join with ss into first sc to create a round.

Round 1: 1sc in each st.

Next round: 1sc in each st until sleeve measures 2¾in (7cm).

Fasten off.

Rep on other side to make second sleeve.

NECKBAND

Rejoin yarn at left front of neck, sc around neck to beginning of right front.

Fasten off.

MAKING UP

Block and press jacket. Sew shoulder seams leaving a neck opening of 1¾in (3.5cm). Turn lapels out and press.

Fasten off.

Stitch down lapels onto front of jacket. Using E, embroider 3 buttons using French knots.

Tip: It is very important to block or press the jacket with a damp cloth.

BERNARD BIGFOOT

Bernard is huge and smelly and thuds around a barnyard near Yosemite. He looks after cows and grunts at everyone. He's a big softie at heart, loves chocolate, and is a chicken fancier.

MATERIALS

Acrylic light worsted (DK) yarn:

Legs, Body, Head, Arms: 1 × 3½oz (100g) balls—approx 306yd (280m)— of light brown (A)

Hair: 1 × 3½oz (100g) balls—approx 306yd (280m)—of dark brown (A)

Eyebrows, Mouth: Small amount of black

Safety eyes

Fiberfill stuffing

Crochet hook size: E/4 (3.5mm) and D/3 (3mm)

ABBREVIATIONS

Beg beginning

Ch chain

Cont continue

Rep repeat

Sc single crochet

Sc2tog *insert hook into next st and draw up a loop; rep from * once, yarn over, draw through all 3 loops on hook.

Ss slip stitch

St(s) stitch(es)

Tog together

SIZE

Approx height: 12in (30cm)

LEGS, BODY & HEAD

Right foot & leg:

Using E/4 (3.5mm) hook and A, make 6ch.

Round 1: 2sc in second ch from hook. 1sc in each of next 3ch, 3sc in last ch. Working on other side of chain, 1sc in each of next 3ch, 2sc in last ch. (14 sts)

Cont working in back of loops only.

Round 2: 1sc in each st. (14 sts)

Round 3: 1sc in each of next 4 sts, sc2tog twice, 1sc in each of last 6 sts. (12 sts)

Round 4: 1sc in each of next 3 sts, sc2tog, 1sc, sc2tog, 1sc in each of last 4 sts. (10 sts)

Round 5: 1sc in each of next 2 sts, sc2tog, 1sc in next st, sc2tog, 1sc in each of last 3 sts. (8 sts)

Begin working in both loops.

Rounds 6–10: 1sc in each st. (8 sts)

Round 11: [1sc in each of next 2 sts, 2sc in next st] twice, 1sc in each of last 2 sts. (10 sts)

Rounds 12–17: 1sc in each st.

Fasten off.

Left leg:

Repeat first foot and leg. Do not fasten off before stuffing.

Stuff legs. Pin legs together with long quilting pins, so both feet are facing in same direction.

Body:

Cont in A, insert hook into unfastened-off st on second leg. Mark beg of round into first st with st marker.

Round 1: 1sc in each of next 5 sts around leg towards back. Insert hook into corresponding st of other leg. Join legs tog by making 1sc in each of next 10 sts of first leg, make 1sc into each of next 5 sts of second leg. (20 sts)

Rounds 2–13: 1sc in each st. (20 sts)

Round 14: *1sc, sc2tog; rep from * to last 2 sts, 1sc in each st. (14 sts)

Round 15: Rep Round 14. (10 sts)

Stuff body.

Do not fasten off.

Head:

Cont using A.

Round 1: 1sc in each st. (10 sts)

Round 2: *1sc in next st, 2sc in next st; rep from * to end of round. (15 sts)

Round 3: *1sc in each of next 2 sts, 2sc in next st; rep from * to end of round. (20 sts)

Round 4: *1sc in each of next 3 sts, 2sc in next st; rep from * to end of round. (25 sts)

Rounds 5–9: 1sc in each st. (25 sts)

Round 10: *1sc in next st, sc2tog; rep from * to end of round. (17 sts)

Insert safety eyes and stuff head.

Round 11: *1sc in next st, sc2tog; rep from * to last 2 sts, sc2tog. (11 sts)

Round 12: Sc2tog around.

Fasten off.

ARMS (make 2)

Using E/4 (3.5mm) hook and A, make 2ch,
  5sc in second ch from hook.
Round 1: *1sc in next st, 2sc in next st; rep
  from * once, 1sc in last st. (7 sts)
Next row: 1sc in each st until arm measures
  3½in (9cm).
Fasten off.

MAKING UP

Do not stuff arms, pin and sew to body.
Embroider mouth and eyebrows.

HEAD & FACE HAIR

Cut several lengths of B each approx 3in
(7.5cm). Using D/3 (3mm) hook, fold each
strand of yarn in half, one at a time, and loop
strands into sts on head and face to create
hair, mustache, and beard.

BODY HAIR

Cut several lengths of B each approx 3in (7.5cm).
Using D/3 (3mm) hook, fold each strand of
yarn in half, one at a time, and loop strands
into each st of body, legs and arms until doll
looks very hairy. Trim as necessary.

WALTER THE WEREWOLF

Walter comes alive at the full moon, when he runs around the woods howling loudly and scaring everyone in the village. He always wakes from these adventures feeling surprisingly well, but can't ever find his clothes.

MATERIALS

Pure wool light worsted (DK) yarn:
Head, Muzzle, Ears, Legs, Body, Arms, Tail:
1 x 1¾oz (50g) ball—approx 124yd (112.5m)—of light brown (A)
Hair: ¼ x 1¾oz (50g) ball—approx 31yd (28.5m)—of dark brown (B)
Blood: Small amount of red (C)
Safety eyes
Fiberfill stuffing
Mouth, Eyebrows, Fingers, Toes: Black embroidery floss
Tongue: Small piece pink felt
Crochet hook sizes: F/5 (4mm) and D/3 (3.25mm)

ABBREVIATIONS

Beg beginning
Ch chain
Rep repeat
Sc single crochet
Sc2tog *insert hook into next st and draw up a loop; rep from * once, yarn over; draw through all 3 loops on hook.
Ss slip stitch
St(s) stitch(es)

SIZE

Approx height: 10in (25cm)

HEAD

Using F/5 (4mm) hook and A, make 2ch, 6sc in second ch from hook.
Round 1: 2sc in each st. (12 sts)
Round 2: *1sc in each of next 2 sts, 2sc in next st; rep from * to end of round. (16 sts)
Round 3: *1sc in each of next 3 sts, 2sc in next st; rep from * to end of round. (20 sts)
Round 4: *1sc in each of next 4 sts, 2sc in next st; rep from * to end of round. (24 sts)
Rounds 5–7: 1sc in each st.
Round 8: *1sc in each of next 2 sts, sc2tog; rep from * to end of round. (18 sts)
Round 9: *1sc in next st, sc2tog; rep from * to end of round. (12 sts)
Insert safety eyes and stuff head.
Round 10: *Sc2tog until opening is closed.
Fasten off.

MUZZLE

Using F/5 (4mm) hook and A, make 2ch, 6sc in second ch from hook.
Round 1: 2sc in each st. (12 sts)
Rounds 2–6: 1sc in each st.
Fasten off.

EARS (make 2)

Using F/5 (4mm) hook and A, make 2ch, 6sc in second ch from hook.
Round 1: 1sc in each st.
Round 2: 2sc in each st. (12 sts)
Rounds 3–4: 1sc in each st. (12 sts)
Round 5: *Sc2tog, 1sc in each of next 4 sts; rep from * to end of round. (10 sts)
Fasten off.

FEET, LEGS & BODY

Right foot & leg:

Using F/5 (4mm) hook and A, make 6ch.
Round 1: 2sc in second ch from hook. 1sc in each of next 3ch, 3sc in last ch. Working on other side of ch, 1sc in each of next 3ch, 2sc in last ch. (14 sts)
Round 2: 1sc in each st. (14 sts)
Round 3: 1sc in each of next 4 sts, sc2tog twice, 1sc in each of last 6 sts. (12 sts)
Round 4: 1sc in each of next 3 sts, sc2tog, 1sc, sc2tog, 1sc in each of last 4 sts. (10 sts)
Round 5: 1sc in each of next 2 sts, sc2tog, 1sc, sc2tog, 1sc in each of last 3 sts. (8 sts)
Rounds 6–17: 1sc in each st. (8 sts)
Fasten off.

Left foot & leg:

Repeat first foot and leg. Do not fasten off before stuffing.
Stuff legs and pin together with long quilting pins, so both feet are facing in same direction.

Body:

Using A, insert hook into unfastened-off st on second leg. Mark beg of round into first st with st marker.
Round 1: 1sc in each of next 4 sts around leg towards back. Pick up first leg and insert hook into corresponding st of first leg. Join legs together by making 1sc in each of next 10 sts of first leg, make 1sc into each of next 2 sts of second leg. (16 sts)
Do not fasten off.
Rounds 2–3: 1sc in each st. (16 sts)
Round 4: 2sc in next st, 1sc in each of next 6 sts, sc2tog, 1sc in each of next 8 sts. (18 sts)

Round 5: 1sc in each of next 2 sts, 2sc in next st, 1sc in each of next 7 sts, 2sc in next st, 1sc in each st to end of round. (20 sts)

Rounds 6–13: 1sc in each st. (20 sts)

Round 14: *1sc, sc2tog; rep from * to last 2 sts, 1sc in each st. (14 sts)

Round 15: Rep Round 14. (10 sts)

Stuff body.

Round 16: Sc2tog until opening is closed.

Fasten off.

ARMS (make 2)

Using F/5 (4mm) hook and A, make 2ch, 5sc into second ch from hook.

Round 1: 2sc in each st. (10 sts)

Round 2: 1sc in each st.

Round 3: *1sc in each of next 3 sts, sc2tog; rep from * to end of round. (8 sts)

Round 4: 1sc in each st until work measures approx 3¼in (8cm).

Fasten off, leaving a long tail for sewing up.

TAIL

Using F/5 (4mm) hook and A, make 2ch, 5sc in second ch from hook.

Round 1: *2sc in next st, 1sc in next st; rep from * once more, 1sc in last st. (7 sts)

Round 2: *1sc in next st, 2sc in next st; rep from * twice, 1sc in last st. (10 sts)

Rounds 3–7: 1sc in each st. (10 sts)

Round 8: *Sc2tog, 1sc in each of next 2 sts; rep from * once, 1sc in each of last 2 sts. (7 sts)

Rounds 9–10: 1sc in each st. (7 sts)

Fasten off.

MAKING UP

Lightly stuff muzzle, pin and sew to face. Embroider nose and mouth details. Cut out pink felt tongue and sew in place just underneath mouth. Embroider eyebrows.

Make a running stitch around inside edge of ears up three sides only, leaving base open, to define the shape. Gently push finger up through gap to open ears and shape, pin and sew to head.

Sew in ends and stuff arms. Pin and sew arms to body. Embroider fingers and toes.

Pin and sew tail to body.

HAIR

Using B, cut several strands of yarn approx 6in (15cm) long. Loop each strand with a small hook around head to create hair, and then trim, leaving the top longer to style into a Mohican. Cut smaller strands for hairy chest, back, hands, feet, and underarms.

BLOOD

Using D/3 (3.25mm) hook, join in C at corner of mouth.

*Make 8ch, ss into fourth ch from hook.

Fasten off.

Sew in end right down to base of ch.

Rejoin yarn into another st; rep from * once more next to first blood droplets but using 10ch to make a longer droplet. Rep on other side of mouth.

Sew in ends carefully.

CHAPTER 3
THE LIVING DEAD

The Living Dead are hanging out in the graveyard.
Lucifer and Witchy Woo are gathering poisonous
potions and Tink the Three-headed Dog is hiding behind
a rock. Natty the Batty is looking for action and is
helping Mr Pumpkin Head try to get Bubbles out of
trouble. Derek the Devil is listening to some old
crooner's tunes and Colin has just bitten the head
off a live, juicy baby chick—again!

MATERIALS

Pure wool light worsted (DK) yarn:

Head, Wart: ½ × 1¾oz (50g) ball—approx 62yd (56m)—of off-white (A)

Shoes: Small amount of green (B)

Legs: Small amount of red (C)

Knickers: ⅛ × 1¾oz (50g) ball—approx 15.5yd (14m)—of pale pink (D)

Body, Arms, Hair, Hat: 1 × 1¾oz (50g) ball—approx 124yd (112.5m)—of black (E)

Eye surrounds: Purple felt

Safety eyes

Fiberfill stuffing

Blackhead: Black embroidery floss

Wart crust: Green embroidery floss

Dress: Approx 9 × 9in (23 × 23cm) piece of black fabric

Cloak: Approx 16 × 7in (41 × 18cm) piece of sparkly gold fabric

Cloak ties: Small piece of black thin ribbon

Broomstick handle: Wooden skewer approx 4½in (11cm)

Broom: Approx 14 strips of leather, around ⅛ × 1½in (0.3 × 4cm)

Crochet hook size: E/4 (3.5mm)

ABBREVIATIONS

Beg beginning

Ch chain

Cont continue

Rep repeat

Sc single crochet

Sc2tog *insert hook into next st and draw up a loop; rep from * once, yarn over, draw through all 3 loops on hook.

Ss slip stitch

St(s) stitch(es)

SIZE

Approx height: 10½in (27cm)

WITCHY WOO

Witchy Woo gave up a promising career in teaching when she realized she could turn naughty children into slugs rather than shout herself hoarse. Now she runs an Internet social network site where young wizards can swap spells and incantations.

HEAD

Using A, make 2ch, 6sc in second ch from hook.

Round 1: 2sc in each st. (12 sts)

Round 2: *1sc in next st, 2sc in next st; rep from * to end of round. (18 sts)

Round 3: *1sc in each of next 2 sts, 2sc in next st; rep from * to end of round. (24 sts)

Rounds 4–8: 1sc in each st. (24 sts)

Round 9: *1sc in each of next 2 sts, sc2tog; rep from * to end of round. (18 sts)

Round 10: *1sc in next st, sc2tog; rep from * to end of round. (12 sts)

Cut small circles of felt, pierce center and insert safety eyes. Insert eyes into head. Stuff head.

Round 11: Sc2tog around.

Fasten off.

SHOES, LEGS & BODY

First shoe & right leg:

Using B, make 6ch.

Round 1: 2sc in second ch from hook. 1sc in each of next 3ch, 3sc in last ch. Working on other side of chain, 1sc in each of next 3ch, 2sc in last ch. (14 sts)

Cont working in back of loops only.

Round 2: 1sc in each st. (14 sts)

Round 3: 1sc in each of next 4 sts, sc2tog twice, 1sc in each of last 6 sts. (12 sts)

Round 4: 1sc in each of next 3 sts, sc2tog, 1sc, sc2tog, 1sc in each of last 4 sts. (10 sts)

Change to C and begin working in both loops.

Rounds 5–15: 1sc in each st. (10 sts)

Stuff leg and sew in ends.

Fasten off.

Second shoe & left leg:

Rep first shoe and leg. Do not fasten off before stuffing.

Stuff legs and pin together with long quilting pins, so that both feet are facing in the same direction.

Knickers:

Using D, insert hook into unfastened-off st on second leg. Mark beg of round into first st with st marker.

Round 1: 1sc in each of next 5 sts around leg towards back. Insert hook into corresponding st of other leg. Join legs tog by making 1sc in each of next 10 sts of first leg, make 1sc into each of next 5 sts of second leg. (20 sts)

Rounds 2–5: 1sc in each st. (20 sts)

Do not fasten off.

Body:

Change to E.

Rounds 6–13: 1sc in each st. (20 sts)

Round 14: *1sc, sc2tog; rep from * to last 2 sts, 1sc in each st. (14 sts)

Round 15: Rep Round 14. (10 sts)

Stuff body.

Round 16: Sc2tog around until opening is closed.

Fasten off.

ARMS (make 2)

Using E, make 2ch, 5sc in second ch from hook.

Round 1: *1sc in next st, 2sc in next st; rep from * once, 1sc in last st. (7 sts)

Next round: 1sc in each st.

Cont making 1sc in each st until arm measures approx 3in (8cm).

Fasten off.

MAKING UP

Stuff arms lightly, pin, and sew to body. Hand sew felt eye surrounds in place. Embroider mouth. Using A, make a large French knot for wart. Make two French knots in black embroidery floss for blackhead and green embroidery floss for wart crust.

HAIR

Cut several strands of E each approx 4in (10cm) long. Place several strands across top of doll's head in a horizontal direction and sew back stitches from forehead to back of neck to secure strands in place.

DRESS

Fold cotton fabric and place dress template on page 110 with shoulders at folded edge. Cut out dress shape. With WS facing, sew sleeve and side seams. Sew sleeve, neck, and bottom hems. Turn right side out and fit on doll.

CLOAK

Pin cloak fabric to fit length on doll and make a small hem along each side. Gather top and hand sew a ribbon on each top corner. Attach cloak to doll.

HAT

Using E, make 2ch, 6ch in second ch from hook.
Round 1: 2sc in each st. (12 sts)
Round 2: *1sc in next st, 2sc in next st; rep from * to end of round. (18 sts)
Rounds 3–6: 1sc in each st. (18 sts)
Round 7: 2sc in each st. (36 sts)
Round 8: Sc2tog around. (18 sts)
Round 9: *1sc in next st, 2sc in next st; rep from * to end of round. (27 sts)
Round 10: *1sc in each of next 2 sts, 2sc in next st; rep from * to end of round. (36 sts)
Round 11: *1sc in each of next 3 sts, 2sc in next st; rep from * to last st, ss into first st from previous round. (45 sts)
Fasten off.
Stuff top of hat with black wool or dark color stuffing and attach to witch's head.

BROOMSTICK

Cover stick by wrapping with E and securing end in place. Attach approx 14 strips of leather and tie with E onto end of broomstick.

LUCIFER THE WITCH'S CAT

The witch put a spell on Lucifer's mouth. He can't talk any more and has to keep his teeth on the collar around his neck. He loves to help Witchy Woo brew up smelly bright green potions in her cauldron.

MATERIALS

Pure wool light worsted (DK) yarn:
Head, Body, Arms, Legs, Ears: ½ × 1¾oz (50g) ball—approx 60yd (55m)—of black (A)
Whiskers: Small amount of white (B)
Safety eyes
Fiberfill stuffing
Nose: Small pieces gray and black felt
Mouth: Black embroidery floss
Collar: Red felt
Teeth: 6 tooth-shaped beads
Small bell
Crochet hook size: F/5 (4mm)

ABBREVIATIONS

Ch chain
Rem remaining
Rep repeat
Sc single crochet
Sc2tog *insert hook into next st and draw up a loop; rep from * once, yarn over, draw through all 3 loops on hook.
Ss slip stitch
St(s) stitch(es)

SIZE

Approx height: 6in (15cm)

HEAD

Using A, make 2ch, 6sc in second chain from hook.
Round 1: 2sc in each st. (12 sts)
Round 2: *1sc in next st, 2sc in next st; rep from * to end of round. (18 sts)
Round 3: *1sc in each of next 2 sts, 2sc in next st; rep from * to end of round. (24 sts)
Rounds 4–10: 1sc in each st. (24 sts)
Round 11: *1sc in each of next 2 sts, sc2tog; rep from * to end of round. (18 sts)
Round 12: 1sc in each st. (18 sts)
Round 13: *1sc in next st, sc2tog; rep from * to end of round. (12 sts)
Insert safety eyes and stuff firmly.
Fasten off, sew in ends.

BODY

Using A, make 2ch, 6sc in second chain from hook.
Round 1: 2sc in each st. (12 sts)
Round 2: *1sc, 2sc in next st; rep from * to end. (18 sts)
Rounds 3–10: 1sc in each st.
Round 11: *1sc in first st, sc2tog; rep from * to end. (12 sts)
Fasten off.

ARMS (make 2)

Using A, make 2ch, 6sc in second chain from hook.
Rounds 1–5: 1sc in each st.
Fasten off leaving long tail.

LEGS (make 2)

Using A, make 2ch, 6sc in second chain from hook.
Rounds 1–4: 1sc in each st.
Fasten off, leaving long tail.

EARS (make 2)

Using A, make 5ch.
Row 1: 1sc in each ch, turn. (4 sts)
Row 2: 1ch, 1sc in each st, turn. (4 sts)
Rep Row 2 twice more, or until you have a square.
Fold square and sc two sides together. At top point make 3ch into same st and continue down second edge. Fasten off.

MAKING UP

Stuff body, pin, and sew to head. Pin and sew arms and legs to body (do not stuff). Pin and sew ears to head. Using B, embroider whiskers.

NOSE

Cut a small circle of gray felt. Cut a small triangular piece of black felt. Sew the black felt onto the gray circle. Embroider mouth. Hand sew in place on cat's face.

COLLAR

Cut a strip of red felt approx ¼ × 5in (0.5 × 12.5cm). Sew on the bead teeth and the small bell. Attach collar around cat's neck.

DEREK THE DEVIL

Derek is 82, which is young for a devil, but he has an array of devilish tricks. He lures women into feeling sorry for him because he's old and then invites them to look around pretty botanical gardens for a "nice day out." He plays Frank Sinatra all the way there and soul on the way back—but he doesn't have good intentions.

MATERIALS

Pure wool light worsted (DK) yarn:
Legs, Body, Head, Arms, Tail, Horns:
  1 x 1¾oz (50g) ball—approx 124yd
  (112.5m)—of red (A)
Fiberfill stuffing
Eye shapes: Black felt
Eye: Flat-back red bead
Eyebrows, teeth: Black embroidery floss
Mouth: White felt
Goatee: Black yarn
Cloak: Approx 7 x 8in (17.5 x 20cm) piece
  of red fabric
Crochet hook size: E/4 (3.5mm) and
  D/3 (3mm)

ABBREVIATIONS

Beg beginning
Ch chain
Cont continue
Rep repeat
Sc single crochet
Sc2tog *insert hook into next st and draw
  up a loop; rep from * once, yarn over,
  draw through all 3 loops on hook.
Ss slip stitch
St(s) stitch(es)

SIZE

Approx height: 9in (23cm)

FEET, LEGS, BODY & HEAD

Right foot & leg:
Using E/4 (3.5mm) hook and A, make 6ch.
Round 1: 2sc in second ch from hook. 1sc in
  each of next 3ch, 3sc in last ch. Working on
  other side of chain, 1sc in each of next 3ch,
  2sc in last ch. (14 sts)
Insert st marker onto loop on hook.
Cont working in back of loops only.
Round 2: 1sc in each st. (14 sts)
Round 3: 1sc in next 4 sts, sc2tog twice, 1sc in
  next 6 sts. (12 sts)
Round 4: 1sc in next 3 sts, sc2tog, 1sc, sc2tog,
  1sc in next 4 sts. (10 sts)
Round 5: 1sc in next 2 sts, sc2tog, 1sc, sc2tog,
  1sc in next 3 sts. (8 sts)
Begin working in both loops.
Rounds 6–10: 1sc in each st. (8 sts)
Round 11: [1sc in each of next 2 sts, 2sc in next
  st] twice, 1sc in each of last 2 sts. (10 sts)
Rounds 12–17: 1sc in each st.
Fasten off.

Left foot & leg:
Rep first foot and leg. Do not fasten off
  before stuffing.
Stuff legs and pin together with long quilting
  pins, so that both feet are facing in the
  same direction.

Body:
Using A, insert E/4 (3.5mm) hook into
  unfastened-off st on second leg. Mark beg of
  round into first st with st marker.
Round 1: 1sc in each of next 5 sts around
  leg towards the back. Insert hook into
  corresponding st of other leg. Join legs tog by
  making 1sc in each of next 10 sts of first leg,
  make 1sc into each of next 5 sts of second
  leg. (20 sts)
Rounds 2–13: 1sc in each st. (20 sts)
Round 14: *1sc, sc2tog; rep from * to last
  2 sts, 1sc in each st. (14 sts)
Round 15: Rep Round 14. (10 sts)
Stuff body.
Do not fasten off.

Head:
Cont using A and E/4 (3.5mm) hook.
Round 1: 1sc in each st. (10 sts)
Round 2: *1sc in next st, 2sc in next st; rep
  from * to end of round. (15 sts)
Round 3: *1sc in each of next 2 sts, 2sc in next
  st; rep from * to end of round. (20 sts)
Round 4: *1sc in each of next 3 sts, 2sc in next
  st; rep from * to end of round. (25 sts)
Rounds 5–9: 1sc in each st. (25 sts)
Round 10: *1sc in next st, sc2tog; rep from
  * to end of round. (17 sts)
Stuff head.
Round 11: *1sc in next st, sc2tog; rep from
  * to last 2 sts, sc2tog. (11 sts)
Round 12: Sc2tog around.
Fasten off.

ARMS (make 2)

Using A and E/4 (3.5mm) hook, make 2ch, 5sc in second ch from hook.

Round 1: *1sc in next st, 2sc in next st; rep from * once, 1sc in last st. (7 sts)

Next round: Work 1sc in each st around, until arm measures 3½in (9cm).

Fasten off. Do not stuff.

TAIL

Using A and E/4 (3.5mm) hook, make 2ch, 2sc in second ch from hook.

Row 1: 2sc in each st. (4 sts)

Row 2: 2sc in first st, 1sc in each of next 2 sts, 2sc in last st. (6 sts)

Row 3: Ss in each of first 2 sts, 1sc in each of next 2 sts, turn.

Row 4: 1sc in each of next 2 sts. (2 sts)

Rep Row 4 until tail measures approx 4½in (12cm).

Fasten off.

HORNS (make 2)

Using A and D/3 (3mm) hook, make 6ch.

Row 1: 1sc in second ch from hook and in each ch to end. (5 sts)

Row 2: Skip 1 st, 1sc in each st to end. (4 sts)

Row 3: Skip 1 st, 1sc in each st to end. (3 sts)

Row 4: Skip 1 st, 1sc in each st to end. (2 sts)

Row 5: Skip 1 st, 1sc in each st to end. (1 st)

Fasten off, leaving a long tail of approx 6in (15cm).

MAKING UP

Pin and sew arms to body. Bend one arm and attach to waist.

Sew tail in place. Fold horn pieces in half lengthways and use yarn tail to sew together, starting at narrow end. Sew in ends.

Cut out eye shapes using templates on page 108 and hand sew to face. Stick red eye bead onto one eye shape. Embroider eyebrows using black yarn. Using mouth template, cut a piece of white felt for mouth and embroider teeth using black embroidery floss. Sew mouth onto face.

GOATEE

Cut approx 4 lengths of black yarn each about 2in (5cm). Fold yarn in half and loop strands underneath mouth on chin area. Trim.

CLOAK

Make a small hem along each side of cloak fabric. Gather top and hand sew onto doll.

TINK THE THREE-HEADED DOG

Tink is the direct descendant of Cerberus, who guarded the gates of Hell. Tink is not much of a guard dog, though—his three heads confuse him and rebel against each other. They spend too much time on their hair and going out to be any use at anyone's gate. They are all always hungry even though they only have one stomach between them.

MATERIALS

Cashmere/merino light worsted (DK) yarn:
Heads, Body, Legs, Tail: 1 × 1¾oz (50g) ball—approx 137yd (125m)—of deep brown (A)
Noses: Scrap of black (B)
Hair: Small amount of light brown, yellow, pink, white
3 sets safety eyes
Fiberfill stuffing
Mouth 1: Small piece white felt, black embroidery floss, pink embroidery floss
Mouth 2: Small piece pale pink felt, red fiber tip pen
Mouth 3: Small piece white felt
Eye surrounds: Scraps of orange, red, gold felt
Crochet hook size: E/4 (3.5mm)

ABBREVIATIONS

Ch chain
Rep repeat
Sc single crochet
Sc2tog *insert hook into next st and draw up a loop; rep from * once, yarn over, draw through all 3 loops on hook.
Ss slip stitch
St(s) stitch(es)

SIZE

Approx height: 4½in (11.5cm)
Approx length: 8in (21cm)

HEADS (make 3)

Using A, make 2ch, 6sc in second ch from hook.
Round 1: 2sc in each st. (12 sts)
Round 2: *1sc in each of next 2 sts, 2sc in next st; rep from * to end of round. (16 sts)
Round 3: *1sc in each of next 3 sts, 2sc in next st; rep from * to end of round. (20 sts)
Round 4: *1sc in each of next 4 sts, 2sc in next st; rep from * to end of round. (24 sts)
Rounds 5–7: 1sc in each st.
Round 8: *1sc in each of next 2 sts, sc2tog; rep from * to end of round. (18 sts)
Round 9: *1sc in each of next 2 sts, sc2tog; rep from * to end of round. (14 sts)
Cut out small circles of felt. Make a small hole in the center and insert safety eyes. Insert eyes into head. Stuff head.
Round 10: Sc2tog until opening is closed.
Fasten off.

MUZZLE (make 3)

Make 2ch, 6sc in second ch from hook.
Round 1: 2sc in each st. (12 sts)
Rounds 2–3: 1sc in each st.
Fasten off.

EARS (make 2 for each head)

Make 2ch, 6sc in second ch from hook.
Round 1: 1sc in each st.
Round 2: 2sc in each st. (12 sts)
Rounds 3–4: 1sc in each st. (12 sts)
Rounds 5: *Sc2tog, 1sc in each of next 4 sts; rep from * to end of round. (10 sts)
Fasten off.

BODY

Make 2ch, 6sc in second chain from hook.
Round 1: 2sc in each st. (12 sts)
Round 2: *1sc in next st, 2sc in next st; rep from * to end of round. (18 sts)
Round 3: *1sc in each of next 2 sts, 2sc in next st; rep from * to end of round. (24 sts)
Round 4: *1sc in each of next 3 sts, 2sc in next st; rep from * to end of round. (30 sts)
Rounds 5–16: 1sc in each st.
Round 17: *1sc in each of next 3 sts, sc2tog; rep from * to end of round. (24 sts)
Round 18: *1sc in each of next 2 sts, sc2tog; rep from * to end of round. (18 sts)
Stuff firmly.
Round 19: *1sc in next st, sc2tog; rep from * to end of round.
Round 20: Sc2tog until gap closes.
Fasten off, sew in ends.

LEGS (make 4)

Make 2ch, make 5sc in second ch from hook.
Round 1: 2sc in each st. (10 sts)
Round 2: 1sc in each st.
Round 3: *1sc in each of next 3 sts, sc2tog; rep from * to end of round. (8 sts)
Round 4: 1sc in each st until work measures approx 1½in (4cm).
Fasten off, leaving a long tail for sewing up.

TAIL

Make 2ch, 5sc in second ch from hook.

Round 1: 2sc in next st, 1sc in each st to last st, 2sc in last st. (7 sts)

Round 2: *1sc in first st, 2sc in next st; rep from * twice more, 1sc in last st. (10 sts)

Rounds 3–6: 1sc in each st.

Round 7: *Sc2tog, 1sc in next 2 sts; rep from * once, sc2tog. (7 sts)

Rounds 8–9: 1sc in each st.

Fasten off.

MAKING UP

Hand sew felt eye surrounds to each dog's face using sewing thread. Lightly stuff each muzzle, pin and sew muzzles to faces. Embroider noses.

Pin and sew ears to each head. Make a running stitch around inside edge of each ear up three sides only, leaving base open. Gently push finger up through gap to open ears and define shape.

Pin and sew head to body.

Stuff legs firmly, pin in position and sew to body.

Stuff tail lightly, pin and sew to body.

MOUTHS

Mouth 1: Cut the shape of a mouth in white felt. Sew in place under dog's nose. Embroider teeth using black embroidery floss and mouth using pink embroidery floss.

Mouth 2: Cut out shape of tongue in pink felt. Color top of tongue using red felt pen. Sew in place under dog's nose.

Mouth 3: Cut small triangles in white felt and sew fangs in place.

HAIR

Style each dog with different hair, cutting yarn and threading it in place by folding short lengths of yarn in half and looping them through the head using a crochet hook. Trim to style.

MR PUMPKIN HEAD

Pete Pumpkin Head's orange swollen head was an unfortunate accident. He was a lovely child, but he was far too interested in organic gardening than was good for him and woke up one day to find the result of all his hard work had quite gone to his head—literally. The only consolation is that he's a really great guy to have around at Halloween.

MATERIALS

Pure wool light worsted (DK) yarn:
Head: 1 × 1¾oz (50g) ball—approx 124yd (112.5m)—of orange (A)
Stalk, Scarf: Small amount of green (B)
Boots: Small amount of gray (C)
Pants: ¼ × 1¾oz (50g) ball—approx 31yd (28.5m)—of blue (D)
Body, Arms: ¼ × 1¾oz (50g) ball—approx 31yd (28.5m)—of brown (E)
Sweater: ½ × 1¾oz (50g) ball—approx 62yd (56.5m)—of gold (F)
Fiberfill stuffing
Face details: Small pieces black felt
Crochet hook size: D/3 (3.25mm)

ABBREVIATIONS

Beg beginning
Ch chain
Cont continue
Dc double crochet
Hdc half double
Rep repeat
Sc single crochet
Sc2tog *insert hook into next st and draw up a loop; rep from * once, yarn over, draw through all 3 loops on hook.
Ss slip stitch
St(s) stitch(es)
Tog together

SIZE

Approx height: 9in (23cm)

HEAD

Head is worked in rows, not rounds. Work all sts in back loops only.
Using A, make 16ch (foundation chain).
Row 1: 1sc in second ch from hook, 1sc in each of next 2 ch, 1hdc in each of next 9 ch, 1sc in each of last 3 ch, turn. (15 sts)
Row 2: 1ch, 1sc in each of next 5 sts, 1hdc in each of next 5 sts, 1sc in each of last 5 sts. (15 sts)
Row 3: 1ch, 1sc in each of next 3 sts, 1hdc in each of next 9 sts, 1sc in each of last 3 sts. (15 sts)
Rows 4–25: Rep Rows 2 and 3 eleven times more. (15 sts)
Row 26: Rep Row 2 once more. (15 sts)
Do not fasten off.
Take hook out of work and fold rectangle in half so foundation chain meets Row 26 (two short sides together). Place hook back into loop and ss through both sides and in each stitch to join seam and form a tube.
Fasten off, leaving a long tail. Turn inside out.

Base:

Thread tapestry needle with long tail. Make small running sts around one open edge to form bottom of head. Pull sts tog, secure yarn tightly to keep end closed. Do not fasten off and keep yarn tail and needle on outside of pumpkin. Stuff head.

Top:

Pass threaded needle up from base of head, through center of stuffing to opening. Make a running st around sts of top opening. Pull sts tog, secure end tightly to keep top closed and sew end in securely.

STALK

Using B, make 2ch, 6sc in second ch from hook.
Rounds 1–6: 1sc in each st. (6 sts)
Round 7: *1sc in next st, 2ch, 1sc in same st; rep from * four times more, 1sc in next st, 2ch, ss in same st.
Fasten off, leaving a long yarn end.

BOOTS, LEGS & BODY

Right boot & leg:

Using C, make 6ch.

Round 1: 2sc in second ch from hook. 1sc in each of next 3ch, 3sc in last ch. Working on other side of chain, 1sc in each of next 3ch, 2sc in last ch. (14 sts)

Cont working in back of loops only.

Round 2: 1sc in each st. (14 sts)

Round 3: 1sc in next 4 sts, sc2tog twice, 1sc in last 6 sts. (12 sts)

Round 4: 1sc in next 3 sts, sc2tog, 1sc, sc2tog, 1sc in last 4 sts. (10 sts)

Round 5: 1sc in next 2 sts, sc2tog, 1sc, sc2tog, 1sc in last 3 sts. (8 sts)

Begin working in both loops.

Rounds 6–9: 1sc in each st. (8 sts)

Change to D and begin working in back loops.

Round 10: 1sc in each st. (8 sts)

Round 11: [1sc in each of next 2 sts, 2sc in next st] twice, 1sc in each of last 2 sts. (10 sts)

Begin working in both loops.

Rounds 12–16: 1sc in each st. (10 sts)

Fasten off.

Boot cuff:

Reattach C at top back of boot into front loop of Round 9.

3ch, *1dc in each front loop around, ss into third of first 3-ch.

Fasten off and sew in end.

Left boot & leg:

Rep first boot and leg. Do not fasten off before stuffing.

Make boot cuff as first leg.

Stuff legs and pin together with long quilting pins, so that both feet are facing in the same direction.

Body:

Using D, make 1sc in each of next 5 sts around second leg. Mark beg of round into first st with st marker.

Round 1: Insert hook into middle st at back of leg. Join legs together by making 1sc in each of next 10 sts of first leg, 1sc into each of next 5 sts of second leg. (20 sts)

Rounds 2–4: 1sc in each st. (20 sts)

Change to E.

Rounds 5–12: 1sc in each st

Round 13: *1sc in next st, sc2tog; rep from * to last 2 sts, 1sc in each st. (14 sts)

Round 14: Rep Row 13. (10 sts)

Stuff body.

Round 15: Sc2tog around until opening is closed. Fasten off.

ARMS (make 2)

Using E, make 2ch, 5sc in second ch from hook.

Round 1: *1sc in next st, 2sc in next st; rep from * once, 1sc in last st. (7 sts)

Round 2: 1sc in each st. (7 sts)

Rep Round 2 until arm measures approx 3in (8cm).

Fasten off.

Tip: Do not overstuff arms or they will not fit into the sweater.

MAKING UP

Pin and sew stalk to top of head, using long yarn end. Cut out pieces of felt using the eye, nose, and mouth templates on page 109 and hand sew to pumpkin face. Stuff arms very lightly, pin and sew to body.

SWEATER

Using F, make 26ch, ss into first ch to form a ring.

Rounds 1–7: 1sc in each st. (26 sts)

Round 8: Sc2tog, 1sc in each of next 12 sts, sc2tog, 1sc in each st to end of round. (24 sts)

Round 9: Sc2tog, 1sc in each of next 11 sts, sc2tog, 1sc in each st to end of round. (22 sts)

Round 10: 1sc in each st. (22 sts)

Fasten off.

First shoulder:

With fasten-off st facing to your right, join yarn into third st in towards center.

Row 1: 1sc in each of next 3 sts. (3 sts)

Row 2: 1sc in each of next 2 sts. (2 sts)

Row 3: Sc2tog. (1 st)

Row 4: 2ch, 2sc in second ch from hook. (2 sts)

Row 5: 1sc in each of next 2 sts. (2 sts)

Row 6: 1sc in next st, 2sc in next st. (3 sts)

Do not fasten off.

Sleeve:

1ch, work 10sc around straight armhole edge, ss in first sc to form a ring.

Place st marker.

Rounds 1–8: 1sc in each st. (10 sts)

Round 9: 2sc in first st, 1sc in each of next 4 sts, 2sc in next st, 1sc in each of last 4 sts. (12 sts)

Round 10: 2sc in first st, 1sc in each of next 5 sts, 2sc in next st, 1sc in each of last 5 sts. (14 sts)

Round 11: 2sc in first st, 1sc in each of next 6 sts, 2sc in next st, 1sc in each of last 6 sts. (16 sts)

Rounds 12–15: 1sc in each st. (16 sts)

Fasten off.

Second shoulder & sleeve:

With fasten-off st facing to your right, skip 1 st and join in F.

Next row: Ss in each st. (3 sts)

Rep first shoulder and sleeve from Row 1, working first 3 sts towards center.

SCARF

Using B, make 45ch, 1hdc in third ch from hook, 1hdc in each ch to end. (43 sts)

Row 1: 2ch, 1hdc in each st to end. (43 sts)

Fasten off.

Attach scarf to Mr Pumpkin Head's neck.

BUBBLES IN TROUBLE

Bubbles has been stabbed—no one knows who did it, but Farmer Modersky has been arrested. Some say it wasn't the farmer and Bubbles jumped over a fence and landed on the carrot. He's been taken to hospital and we're hoping for a speedy recovery.

MATERIALS

Alpaca/silk worsted (Aran) yarn:
Head, Body, Ears, Legs, Arms: 1 × 1¾oz (50g) ball—approx 71yd (65m)—of gray (A)
Tail, Tear: Small amount of white (B)
Carrot: ½ × 1¾oz (50g) ball—approx 35yd (32m)—of orange (C)
Blood: Small amount of red (E)
Mohair yarn:
Carrot top: Small amount of green (D)
Eye surround: Small piece white felt
Black safety eyes
Fiberfill stuffing
Crochet hook size: F/5 (4mm)

ABBREVIATIONS

Beg beginning
Ch chain
Rep repeat
Sc single crochet
Sc2tog *insert hook into next st and draw up a loop; rep from * once, yarn over, draw through all 3 loops on hook.
Ss slip stitch
St(s) stitch(es)

SIZE

Approx height: 11½in (29cm)

RABBIT

HEAD

Using A, make 2ch, 4sc in second ch from hook. (4 sts)
Place st marker at beg of each round (when counting, loop on hook counts as one st).
Round 1: 2sc in each st. (8 sts)
Round 2: *1sc in next st, 2sc in next st; rep from * to end of round. (12 sts)
Rounds 3–4: 1sc in each st.
Round 5: *1sc in each of next 2 sts, 2sc in next st; rep from * to end of round. (16 sts)
Round 6: *1sc in each of next 3 sts, 2sc in next st; rep from * to end of round. (20 sts)
Rounds 7–9: 1sc in each st. (20 sts)
Round 10: *1sc in each of next 3 sts, sc2tog; rep from * to end of round. (16 sts)
Round 11: *1sc in each of next 2 sts, sc2tog; rep from * to end of round. (12 sts)
Cut two small circles in white felt. Make a small hole in each center, push the safety eye through the felt and insert onto face. Stuff head.
Round 12: *1sc in next st, sc2tog; rep from * to end of round. (8 sts)
Round 13: Sc2tog around.
Fasten off, sew in ends.

TAIL

Using B, make a small pompom.

BODY

Using A, make 2ch, 6sc in second chain from hook.
Round 1: 2sc in each st. (12 sts)
Round 2: *1sc in next st, 2sc in next st; rep from * to end of round. (18 sts)
Round 3: *1sc in each of next 2 sts, 2sc in next st; rep from * to end of round. (24 sts)
Round 4: *1sc in each of next 3 sts, 2sc in next st; rep from * to end of round. (30 sts)
Rounds 5–12: 1sc in each st.
Round 13: *1sc in each of next 3 sts, sc2tog; rep from * to end of round. (24 sts)
Round 14: *1sc in each of next 2 sts, sc2tog; rep from * to end of round. (18 sts)
Round 15: 1sc in each st.
Stuff firmly.
Round 16: *1sc in next st, sc2tog; rep from * to end of round.
Round 17: *1sc, sc2tog; rep from * to end of round.
Fasten off, sew in ends.

EARS (make 2)

Using A, make 2ch, 4sc in second ch from hook. (4 sts)
Round 1: *1sc in next st, 2sc in next st; rep once more. (6 sts)
Round 2: *1sc in next st, 2sc in next st; rep twice more. (9 sts)
Round 3: 1sc in each of next 4 sts, 2sc in next st, 1sc in each of next 3 sts, 2sc in last st. (11 sts)
Rounds 4–10: 1sc in each st.
Fasten off.

LEGS (make 2)

Using A, make 2ch, 6sc in second ch from hook.

Round 1: 2sc in each st. (12 sts)

Round 2: *1sc in each of next 2 sts, 2sc in next st; rep from * to end of round. (16 sts)

Rounds 3–4: 1sc in each st.

Round 5: *1sc in each of next 2 sts, sc2tog; rep from * to end of round. (12 sts)

Rounds 6–17: 1sc in each st.

Fasten off.

ARMS (make 2)

Using A, make 2ch, 6sc in second ch from hook.

Round 1: 2sc in each st. (12 sts)

Round 2: *1sc in each of next 2 sts, 2sc in next st; rep from * to end of round. (16 sts)

Rounds 3–4: 1sc in each st.

Round 5: *1sc in each of next 2 sts, sc2tog; rep from * to end of round. (12 sts)

Rounds 6–14: 1sc in each st.

Fasten off.

CARROT

MAIN PART

Using C, make 2ch, make 10sc into second ch from hook.

Round 1: 2sc in each st to end of round. (20 sts)

Round 2: Working in back loops only, 1sc in each st. (20 sts)

Round 3: *1sc in each of next 3 sts, sc2tog; rep from * to end of round. (16 sts)

Round 4: 1sc in each of next 2 sts, sc2tog; rep from * to end of round. (12 sts)

Round 5: *1sc in next st, sc2tog; rep from * to end of round. (8 sts)

Rounds 6–8: 1sc in each st.

Round 9: 1sc in each of next 3 sts, sc2tog, 1sc in each of last 3 sts. (7 sts)

Round 10: 1sc in each of next 2 sts, sc2tog, 1sc in each of last 3 sts. (6 sts)

Fasten off.

TOP

Using D, attach yarn to top main piece of carrot. Make 10ch, ss in next and each ch, ss into next st around top of carrot.

Cont making carrot leaves all around top of carrot. Ss into joining st.

Fasten off.

MAKING UP

Hand sew felt eyes onto head. Using B and embroidery chain st, embroider a tear under one eye. Pin and sew body to head. Make a running stitch around outer edges to make ears lie flat. Pin and sew ears to head. Stuff legs and arms, pin and sew to body. Sew tail to body. Stuff carrot and attach to Rabbit's tummy.

BLOOD

Join E at top of carrot where it has been stitched to body. Make 15ch, ss in fourth ch from hook.

Fasten off leaving long tail.

Using a tapestry needle, sew in end by weaving in and out of chain at back, fasten off into body to secure.

Repeat to make blood droplets around top of carrot.

COLIN THE CANNIBAL COCKEREL

Colin is the loveliest cockerel in the coop. He looks after all his hens carefully and really adores his brood. But sometimes—when the moon is full—he's overcome and seizes a juicy real chicken nugget for a snack. In the morning, he can always blame the fox...

MATERIALS

Pure wool light worsted (DK) yarn:

Head, Body, Wings: ½ × 3½oz (100g) ball —approx 109yd (100m)—of black (A)

Legs, Chick: ¼ × 1¾oz (50g) ball—approx 32yd (29m)—of yellow (B)

Feet, Sole, Eyes: ¼ × 1¾oz (50g) ball —approx 32yd (29m)—of cream (C)

Beak, Chick Legs: ¼ × 3½oz (100g) ball —approx 54yd (50m)—of orange (D)

Head Comb: ½ × 3½oz (100g) ball— approx 109yd (100m)—of red (E)

Teeth: Small amount of white

Feathers: Scraps of light green, purple, light blue, dark blue

Fiberfill stuffing

Safety eyes

Crochet hook sizes: B/1 (2mm), D/3 (3mm) and F/5 (4mm)

ABBREVIATIONS

Ch chain

Dc double crochet

Hdc half double

Foll following

Rep repeat

Sc single crochet

Sc2tog *insert hook into next st and draw up a loop; rep from * once, yarn over, draw through all 3 loops on hook.

Ss slip stitch

St(s) stitch(es)

SIZE

Approx height: 13in (33cm)

COCKEREL

HEAD

Using F/5 (4mm) hook and A, make 2ch, 6sc in second ch from hook. Join with ss to form a ring.

Round 1: 2sc in each st. (12 sts)

Round 2: *1sc in next st, 2sc in next st; rep from * to end of round. (18 sts)

Round 3: *1sc in each of next 2 sts, 2sc in next st; rep from * to end of round. (24 sts)

Round 4: *1sc in each of next 3 sts, 2sc in next st; rep from * to end of round. (30 sts)

Rounds 5–10: 1sc in each st. (30 sts)

Round 11: *2sc in next st; 1sc in each of next 9 sts; rep from * to end of round. (33 sts)

Round 12: 2sc in first st, 1sc in each st to end of round. (34 sts)

Round 13: 1sc in each st. (34 sts)

Round 14: 2sc in first st, 1sc in each st to end of round. (35 sts)

Round 15: 2sc in first st, 1sc in each st to end of round. (36 sts)

Round 16: *Skip 1 st, 3dc in next st, skip 1 st, ss in next st; rep from * to end of round.
Fasten off.

BODY & LEGS

Body:

Using F/5 (4mm) hook and A, make 2ch, 6sc in second ch from hook. Join with ss to form a ring.

Round 1: 2sc in each st. (12 sts)

Round 2: *1sc in next st, 2sc in next st; rep from * to end of round. (18 sts)

Round 3: *1sc in each of next 2 sts, 2sc in next st; rep from * to end of round. (24 sts)

Round 4: *1sc in each of next 3 sts, 2sc in next st; rep from * to end of round. (30 sts)

Round 5: *1sc in each of next 4 sts, 2sc in next st; rep from * to end of round. (36 sts)

Rounds 6–11: 1sc in each st. (36 sts)

Round 12: *Sc2tog, 1sc in each of next 10 sts; rep from * to end of round. (33 sts)

Round 13: 1sc in each st. (33 sts)

Round 14: *Sc2tog, 1sc in each of next 9 sts; rep from * to end of round. (30 sts)

Rounds 15–18: 1sc in each st. (30 sts)

Round 19: *Sc2tog, 1sc in each of next 13 sts; rep from * to end of round. (28 sts)

Round 20: *Sc2tog, 1sc in each of next 12 sts; rep from * to end of round. (26 sts)

Do not fasten off.

First leg:

Join in B.

Round 21: 1sc in each of next 13 sts, skip next 13 sts, join with ss into first sc to form a ring. (13 sts)

Round 22: 1sc, sc2tog, 1sc in each st to end of round. (12 sts)

Round 23: 1sc in each st. (12 sts)

Round 24: 1sc, sc2tog, 1sc in each st to end of round. (11 sts)

Rounds 25–26: 1sc in each st. (11 sts)

Round 27: Put hook into first st and join in C with B. 1sc in each st using both strands. (11 sts)

Round 28: 2sc in each of next 2 sts, 1hdc in each of next 3 sts, 1sc in next 6 sts. (13 sts)

Round 29: 1sc in each of next 2 sts, 1hdc in each of next 3 sts, 1sc in next 7 sts, 1ch, turn.

Rounds 30–33: 1sc in each of next 5 sts, 1ch, turn.

Fasten off.

Second leg:

Join C in sixteenth st of Round 20 (joining place is at side of yarn tail).

Round 1: 1sc in each of next 13 sts, join with ss into first sc to form a ring. (13 sts)

Rep Rounds 22–27 of first leg.

Round 28: 1sc in each of next 8 sts, 1hdc in next 3 sts, 1sc in next 2 sts. (13 sts)

Round 29: Rep Round 28. (13 sts)

Round 30: 1sc in each of next 8 sts, 1ch, turn.

Rounds 31–33: 1sc in each of next 5 sts, 1ch, turn.

Fasten off.

SOLE OF FOOT (make 2)

Using F/5 (4mm) hook and C, make 6ch, 1sc into next ch from hook, 1sc in each st to end. (5 sts)

Row 1: 1ch, 1sc in each st. (5 sts)

Rows 2–7: Rep Round 1.

Row 8: 1ch, sc2tog, 1sc in each of next 3 sts, sc2tog. (3 sts)

Row 9: 1ch, skip 1 st, 1sc in next st, ss in last st.

Fasten off.

BEAK

Top beak:

Using F/5 (4mm) hook and D, make 2ch, 3sc in second ch from hook. Join with ss to form a ring.

Round 1: 2sc in each st. (6 sts)

Round 2: 1sc in each st. (6 sts)

Round 3: 1hdc in each of next 4 sts, 1sc in next 2 sts. (6 sts)

Round 4: *2hdc in next st, 1hdc in next st; rep from * once more, 2sc in next st, 1sc in next st. (9 sts)

Round 5: *2hdc in next st, 1hdc in next st; rep from * once more, 2sc in next st, 1sc in each st to end of round. (12 sts)

Round 6: 1sc in each st. (12 sts)

Round 7: *2sc in next st, 1sc in each of next 3 sts; rep from * to end of round. (15 sts)

Round 8: 1sc in each st. (15 sts)

Fasten off.

Bottom beak:

Using F/5 (4mm) hook and D, make 2ch, 3sc in second ch from hook. Join with ss to form a ring.

Round 1: 2sc in each st. (6 sts)

Round 2: 1sc in each of next 2 sts, 1hdc in each of next 2 sts, 1sc in each of next 2 sts. (6 sts)

Round 3: Rep Round 2, 1ch, turn. (6 sts)

Round 4: 2sc in next st, 1sc in each of next 4 sts, 2sc in last st. (8 sts)

Fasten off.

EYES (make 2)

Using D/3 (3mm) hook and C, and leaving a long end of approx 6in (15cm), make 2ch, 5sc into second ch from hook. Join with ss to form a ring.

Round 1: 1ch, 1sc in next st, 2sc in each st to end, join with ss into first ch.

Round 2: 1ch, 1sc in each st.

Round 3: Sc2tog around.

Fasten off.

WINGS (make 2)

Using F/5 (4mm) hook and A, make 5ch, 1sc in second ch from hook.

Row 1: 1sc in each ch to end. (4 sts)

Row 2: 1ch, 2sc in first st, 1sc in each of next 2 sts, 2sc in last st. (6 sts)

Row 3: 1ch, 2sc in first st, 1sc in each of next 4 sts, 2sc in last st. (8 sts)

Row 4: 1ch, 2sc in first st, 1sc in each of next 6 sts, 2sc in last st. (10 sts)

Row 5: 2ch, 2hdc in first st, 1sc in each of next 8 sts, 2hdc in last st. (12 sts)

Row 6: 3ch, 1dc in each st to end. (12 sts)

Rows 7–8: 3ch, 1dc in each st to end. (12 sts)

Fasten off.

TAIL FEATHERS (make 5 or 6 in assorted colors)

Using F/5 (4mm) hook, make 25ch, 1sc in first ch from hook, 1sc in each st to end. (24 sts)

Working on underside of chains, make 1sc in second ch.

*Turn work over and work on other side (single crochet row from previous round), skip 3 sts, 1sc in next st.

Turn work over again onto underside of chains, make 1sc into third ch along from previous sc on same side; rep from * to end.

Fasten off. Sew in ends.

HEAD COMB (make 3)

Using F/5 (4mm) hook and E, make 2ch, 3sc into second ch from hook.

Round 1: 2sc in each st. (6 sts)

Rounds 2–3: 1sc in each st. (6 sts)

Round 4: *2sc in next st, 1sc in next st; rep from * to end of round. (9 sts)

Round 5: *1sc in each of next 3 sts, 1hdc in each of next 3 sts, 1sc in each of next 3 sts; rep from * to end of round. (9 sts)

Round 6: Rep Round 5. (9 sts)

Round 7: *2sc in next st, 1sc in each of next 2 sts; rep from * to end of round. (12 sts)

Round 8: *2sc in next st, 1sc in each of next 3 sts; rep from * to end of round. (15 sts)

Round 9: 1sc in each st. (15 sts)

Round 10: 1hdc in each of next 5 sts, 1sc in each of next 2 sts, [sc2tog] 3 times, 1sc in each of last 2 sts. (12 sts)

Fasten off.

MAKING UP

Stuff body. Thread a needle and bring first long end of eye through, scrunch up end and push into center of button. Push safety eyes into eye circles and secure. Sew eyes in place onto head. Sew in ends. Stuff head and sew to body above the scalloped edge of neck.

Stuff legs. Sew soles of feet onto each leg. Embroider claws onto feet.

Stuff top part of beak and sew onto head. Sew bottom part of beak to top of beak (should only be sewn at flap created on Round 4 of bottom beak).

Pin and sew wings in place with narrowest end facing towards front.

Attach each tail feather to chicken's rear by sewing them individually but bunched together. Pin and sew head comb onto head in a line from front to back.

TEETH (make 2)

Using B/1 (2mm) hook and white yarn, make 2ch, 2sc in second ch from hook, turn.

1sc in first st, 2sc in last st.

Fold triangle in half and stitch together. Stitch one onto each side of beak.

BABY CHICK

HEAD

Using D/3 (3mm) hook and B, make 2ch, 6sc in second ch from hook.

Round 1: 2sc in each st. (12 sts)

Round 2: *1sc in next st, 2sc in next st; rep from * to end of round. (18 sts)

Rounds 4–7: 1sc in each st. (18 sts)

Round 8: *1sc in next st, sc2tog; rep from * to end of round. (12 sts)

Stuff head lightly.

Round 9: Sc2tog around.

Fasten off.

BODY

Using B, make 2ch, 6sc in second ch from hook.

Round 1: 2sc in each st. (12 sts)

Rounds 2–8: 1sc in each st. (12 sts)

Stuff body lightly.

Round 9: Sc2tog around.

Fasten off.

LEGS (make 2)

Using D, make 6ch, 1hdc in third ch from hook.

Fasten off.

MAKING UP

Sew in ends. Attach head and legs to body. Using A, embroider French knots for eyes. Cut a small square of pink felt, fold in half and trim on each side to beak shape. Sew onto face.

Sew baby chick inside cockerel's mouth.

NATTY THE BATTY

Don't underestimate Natty the Batty. He is small but that makes it easy for him to sneak up on people—he'll sink his fangs into your neck before you can blink.

MATERIALS

Pure wool light worsted (DK) yarn:
Head, Ears, Body, Wings: 1 × 1¾oz (50g) ball—approx 124yd (112.5m)—of gray-blue (A)
Legs, Mouth: Small amount of black (B)
Safety eyes
Fiberfill stuffing
Nose: Light brown and black felt
Fangs: White felt
Crochet hook size: F/5 (4mm)

ABBREVIATIONS

Ch chain
Dc double crochet
Foll follows
Hdc half double
Rep repeat
Sc single crochet
Sc2tog *insert hook into next st and draw up a loop; rep from * once, yarn over, draw through all 3 loops on hook.
Ss slip stitch
St(s) stitch(es)
Tr treble crochet

SIZE

Approx length: 4in (10cm)
Approx wingspan: 6in (15cm)

HEAD

Using A, make 2ch, 6sc in second ch from hook.
Round 1: 2sc in each st. (12 sts)
Round 2: *1sc in next st, 2sc in next st; rep from * to end of round. (18 sts)
Round 3: *1sc in each of next 2 sts, 2sc in next st; rep from * to end of round. (24 sts)
Rounds 4–6: 1sc in each st. (24 sts)
Round 7: *1sc in each of next 2 sts, sc2tog; rep from * to end of round. (18 sts)
Round 8: *1sc in next st, sc2tog; rep from * to end of round. (12 sts)
Insert safety eyes, stuff head.
Round 9: Sc2tog around. (6 sts)
Fasten off.

EARS (make 2)

Using A, make 2ch, 3sc in second ch from hook, turn. (3 sts)
Row 1: 1ch, 2sc in first st, 1sc, 1dc, 1sc in next st, 2sc in last st, turn. (7 sts)
Row 2: 1ch, 2sc in first st, 1sc in each of next 2 sts, 3sc in next st, 1sc in each of next 2 sts, 2sc in last st, turn. (11 sts)
Fasten off.

BODY

Using A, make 2ch, 6sc in second ch from hook.
Round 1: 2sc in each st. (12 sts)
Round 2: *1sc in next st, 2sc in next st; rep from * to end of round. (18 sts)
Round 3: *1sc in each of next 2 sts, 2sc in next st; rep from * to end of round. (24 sts)
Rounds 4–9: 1sc in each st. (24 sts)
Round 10: *1sc in each of next 2 sts, sc2tog; rep from * to end of round. (18 sts)
Stuff body.
Round 11: *1sc in next st, sc2tog; rep from * to end of round. (12 sts)

Round 12: Sc2tog around. (6 sts)
Fasten off.

WINGS (make 2)

Using A, make 2ch, 1sc in first ch.
Row 1: 3sc in st, 1ch. (3 sts)
Row 2: 2sc in next st, 1sc in next st, 1sc and 1dc in last st, 1ch. (5 sts)
Row 3: 2sc in first st, 1sc in each of next 3 sts, 2sc in last st, 1ch. (7 sts)
Row 4: 1sc in each of next 6 sts, 1sc and 1dc in last st, 1ch. (8 sts)
Row 5: 2sc in first st, 1sc in each of next 7 sts, 1ch. (9 sts)
Row 6: 1sc in each of next 3 sts, 1hdc in next st, 1dc, 1tr, 1dc in next st, 1hdc in next st, 1sc in next st, 1hdc, 1dc. 2tr in last st. (13 sts)
Do not fasten off.

Wing edging:

3sc in last st of Row 6 (makes corner). Work down wings as foll: 1sc in base of last tr from prev round, 2sc, ss into dip, 4sc to next corner; 3sc in corner st, 6sc to next corner; 3sc in corner st, 3sc, ss into dip, 5sc, ss into next dip, 4sc, ss into first sc. Fasten off.

LEGS (make 2)

Using B, make 10ch, 1hdc in fourth ch from hook. Fasten off.

MAKING UP

Weave ends through last 6 sts of head to close. Sew body and ears to head. Attach wings three rows behind head. Sew legs to underside of body. Cut circle of brown felt and two smaller ones in black. Sew black circles onto brown and then sew onto nose. Embroider mouth in B. Cut four fangs in white felt and sew in place.

CHAPTER 4
DEATHLY COMPANIONS

Frankenstein's Youngster has given Nobby a nose
bleed, so he won't be rocking tonight. Murderous Mary
has been chasing Dr Death and there is so much blood
even the Tomatoes From the 'Hood have escaped to
hide behind the lettuces. Payne the Goth Girl is trying
to calm down Penelope, who has been vomiting bile all
morning, and Piercing Phyllis is so fed up she's
seriously considering stabbing them both.

MURDEROUS MARY

Mary is a serial killer who only strikes at night. She sneaks out of her bedroom window and stalks the streets looking for her next victim. She loves wearing a nightgown as she likes to be comfortable for her exertions.

MATERIALS

Pure wool light worsted (DK) yarn:
Boots: Small amount of bright pink (A)
Legs, Body, Head, Arms: 1 × 1¾oz (50g) ball—approx 124yd (112.5m)—of beige (B)
Hair: Small amount of yellow (C)
Eye surrounds: Light pink felt
Safety eyes
Fiberfill stuffing
Mouth: Small amount of pale pink
Scar: Red embroidery floss
Dress: Approx 9 × 18in (23 × 45cm) piece of white cotton
Blood: Red yarn and red acrylic paint
Toy knife
Crochet hook size: F/5 (4mm)

ABBREVIATIONS

Beg beginning
Ch chain
Cont continue
Dc double crochet
Rep repeat
Sc single crochet
Sc2tog *insert hook into next st and draw up a loop; rep from * once, yarn over, draw through all 3 loops on hook.
Ss slip stitch
St(s) stitch(es)

SIZE

Approx height: 9½in (24cm)

BOOTS, LEGS & BODY

Right boot & leg:
Using A, make 6ch.
Round 1: 2sc in second ch from hook. 1sc in each of next 3ch, 3sc in last ch. Working on other side of chain, 1sc in each of next 3ch, 2sc in last ch. (14 sts)
Cont working in back of loops only.
Round 2: 1sc in each st. (14 sts)
Round 3: 1sc in each of next 4 sts, sc2tog twice, 1sc in each of last 6 sts. (12 sts)
Round 4: 1sc in each of next 3 sts, sc2tog, 1sc, sc2tog, 1sc in each of last 4 sts. (10 sts)
Round 5: 1sc in each of next 2 sts, sc2tog, 1sc, sc2tog, 1sc in each of last 3 sts. (8 sts)
Cont working in both loops.
Rounds 6–9: 1sc in each st. (8 sts)
Change to B, cont working in back loops.
Round 10: 1sc in each st. (8 sts)
Round 11: [1sc in each of next 2 sts, 2sc in next st] twice, 1sc in each of last 2 sts. (10 sts)
Cont working in both loops.
Rounds 12–16: 1sc in each st.
Fasten off.

Boot cuff:
Attach A into front loop of Round 9, at back of boot top.
Make 3ch, *2dc in each front loop around, ss into third of first 3-ch.
Fasten off and sew in end.

Left boot, leg & boot cuff:
Rep first boot and leg. Do not fasten off before stuffing.
Make boot cuff as first boot.
Stuff legs and pin together with long quilting pins, so that both feet are facing in same direction.

Body:
Using B, make 1sc in each of next 5 sts around second leg. Mark beg of round into first st with st marker.
Round 1: Insert hook into middle st at back of leg. Join legs together by making 1sc in each of next 10 sts of first leg, 1sc into each of next 5 sts of second leg. (20 sts)
Rounds 2–4: 1sc in each st. (20 sts)
Rounds 5–12: 1sc in each st.
Round 13: *1sc in next st, sc2tog; rep from * to last 2 sts, 1sc in each st. (14 sts)
Round 14: Rep Row 13. (10 sts)
Stuff body.
Round 15: Sc2tog around until opening is closed.
Fasten off.

HEAD

Starting at top of head and using B, make 2ch, 6sc in second ch from hook.
Round 1: 2sc in each st. (12 sts)
Round 2: *1sc in next st, 2sc in next st; rep from * to end of round. (18 sts)
Round 3: *1sc in each of next 2 sts, 2sc in next st; rep from to end of round. (24 sts)
Rounds 4–8: 1sc in each st. (24 sts)
Round 9: *1sc in each of next 2 sts, sc2tog; rep from * to end of round. (18 sts)
Round 10: *1sc in next st, sc2tog; rep from * to end of round. (12 sts)

Cut two small felt circles, make a hole in the
center of each and insert safety eyes. Insert
eyes into face. Hand sew felt circles to face.
Stuff carefully, placing most stuffing to bottom of
head and very little at top, so doll has a
slightly square-shape head.

Round 11: 1sc in each st. (12 sts)

Round 12: Sc2tog until opening is closed.
Fasten off.

ARMS (make 2)

Using B, make 2ch, 5sc in second ch from hook.

Round 1: *2sc in next st, 1sc in next st; rep
from * to end. (8 sts)

Rounds 3–11: 1sc in each st. (8 sts)
Fasten off.

MAKING UP

Sew in ends, keeping top of head flat. Pin and
sew head to body. Stuff arms lightly, pin and
sew to body.

Embroider mouth in pink yarn. Using red yarn
for blood, embroider scar and make embroidered chain stitches around head area, with a
few stitches coming from mouth.

HAIR

Using C, thread a tapestry needle and
embroider a fringe and hair to back of doll's
head. Cut 12 strands of C and make a braid
long enough to go from one side of head to
the other. Sew in position.

DRESS

Fold cotton fabric and, using the template on
page 110 with shoulders at the folded edge, cut
out dress shape. With wrong sides facing, sew
sleeve, neck, and bottom hems. Sew along
seams. Turn right side out.

Using red acrylic paint, smear bloodstains onto
dress. When paint is dry, fit dress onto doll.
Attach toy knife in hand.

POSSESSED PENELOPE

Penelope is very jealous, especially of her sister. Recently she found out her sister had been given a new laptop, so Penelope's head swiveled, she turned green, and levitated up to the ceiling.

MATERIALS

Pure wool light worsted (DK) yarn:
Legs, Body, Arms: ½ × 1¾oz (50g) ball
   —approx 68.5yd (62.5m)—of
   off-white (A)
Head: ¼ × 1¾oz (50g) ball—approx 33yd
   (30m)—of green (B)
Hair: ¼ × 1¾oz (50g) ball—approx 33yd
   (30m)—of brown (C)
Fiberfill stuffing
Eye surround: Small piece of black felt
Eyes: 2 × flat-back red beads
Eyebrows: Black yarn or embroidery floss
Mouth: Small piece of light brown felt
Teeth: Mustard embroidery floss
Nightdress: Approx 9 × 18in
   (23 × 45cm) piece lightweight cotton
   fabric
Vomit: Yellow/green acrylic paint
Hair bow: Approx 20in (50cm) fine black
   ribbon
Crochet hook size: F/5 (4mm)

ABBREVIATIONS

Ch chain
Cont continue
Rep repeat
Sc single crochet
Sc2tog *insert hook into next st and draw
   up a loop; rep from * once, yarn over,
   draw through all 3 loops on hook.
Ss slip stitch
St(s) stitch(es)

SIZE

Approx height: 9in (23cm)

FEET, LEGS & BODY

Right foot & leg:
Using A, make 6ch.
Round 1: 2sc in second ch from hook. 1sc in
   each of next 3ch, 3sc in last ch. Working on
   other side of chain, 1sc in each of next 3ch,
   2sc in last ch. (14 sts)
Cont working in back of loops only.
Round 2: 1sc in each st. (14 sts)
Round 3: 1sc in each of next 4 sts, sc2tog twice,
   1sc in each of last 6 sts. (12 sts)
Round 4: 1sc in each of next 3 sts, sc2tog, 1sc,
   sc2tog, 1sc in each of last 4 sts. (10 sts)
Round 5: 1sc in each of next 2 sts, sc2tog, 1sc,
   sc2tog, 1sc in each of last 3 sts. (8 sts)
Begin working in both loops.
Rounds 6–9: 1sc in each st. (8 sts)
Begin working in back loops only.
Round 10: 1sc in each st. (8 sts)
Round 11: [1sc in each of next 2 sts, 2sc in next
   st] twice, 1sc in each of last 2 sts. (10 sts)
Begin working in both loops.
Rounds 12–17: 1sc in each st. (10 sts)
Fasten off.

Left foot & leg:
Rep first foot & leg. Do not fasten off
   before stuffing.
Stuff legs. Pin legs together with long quilting
   pins, so both feet are facing in same direction.

Body:
Cont using A and make 1sc in each of next 5 sts
   around second leg. Mark beg of round into first
   st with st marker.
Round 1: Insert hook into middle st at back of
   leg. Join legs tog by making 1sc in each of next
   10 sts of first leg, 1sc into each of next
   5 sts of second leg. (20 sts)
Rounds 2–12: 1sc in each st. (20 sts)
Round 13: *1sc in next st, sc2tog; rep from
   * to last 2 sts, 1sc in each of last 2 sts. (14 sts)
Round 14: Rep Row 13. (10 sts)
Stuff body.
Round 15: Sc2tog around.
Fasten off.

HEAD

Using B, make 2ch, 6sc in second ch from hook.
Round 1: 2sc in each st. (12 sts)
Round 2: *1sc in next st, 2sc in next st; rep
   from * to end of round. (18 sts)
Round 3: *1sc in each of next 2 sts, 2sc in next
   st; rep from * to end of round. (24 sts)
Rounds 4–6: 1sc in each st.
Round 7: *1sc in each of next 2 sts, sc2tog; rep
   from * to end of round. (18 sts)
Round 8: *1sc in next st, sc2tog; rep from
   * to end of round. (12 sts)
Stuff head.
Round 9: Sc2tog until opening is closed.
Fasten off.

ARMS (make 2)

Using A, make 2ch, 5sc in second ch from hook.

Round 1: *2sc in next st, 1sc in next st; rep from * to last st, 2sc in last st. (8 sts)

Rounds 2–16: 1sc in each st. (8 sts)

Fasten off.

MAKING UP

Stuff arms lightly and sew to body, making sure they are pointing to front in same direction as feet. Cut small disks of black felt and sew onto face as eyes. Stick bead eyes onto felt with strong adhesive. Embroider eyebrows. Cut mouth from light brown felt using the photo opposite as a guide. Using mustard embroidery floss, embroider teeth onto felt. Sew mouth to head. Sew head onto body with face looking to rear.

NIGHTDRESS

Step 1: Fold cotton fabric and using the template on page 110 with shoulders at the folded edge, cut out nightdress shape.

Step 2: With wrong side facing, sew sleeve, neck and bottom hems. Sew seams.

Step 3: Turn nightdress right side out and fit onto doll. Smear green and yellow paint over front of nightdress and down chin as vomit.

HAIR

Cut approx 80 strands of C each 9in (23cm) long. Lay strands horizontally across head at top and down back. Using back stitch, secure down center to create center parting. Tie hair into bunches and secure into a bow using ribbon. Trim hair if necessary.

MATERIALS

Pure wool light worsted (DK) yarn:

Shoes: ¼ × 1¾oz (50g) ball—approx 32yd (29m)—of dark blue (A)

Legs, Body, Head, Arms: ½ × 1¾oz (50g) ball —approx 68.5yd (62.5m)—of beige (B)

Hair, Eyebrows: Scraps of brown (C)

Fiberfill stuffing

Eye surround: Small piece of red felt

Safety eyes

Mask: 1½ ×1in (4 × 2.5cm) piece of lightweight white cotton fabric

Mask ties: Approx 24in (61cm) white embroidery floss

Scrubs: Approx 12 × 12in (30.5 × 30.5cm) piece of lightweight blue cotton fabric

Tools: Miniature toy knives and axes

Blood: Red acrylic paint

Crochet hook size: F/5 (4mm)

ABBREVIATIONS

Beg beginning

Ch chain

Cont continue

Rep repeat

Sc single crochet

Sc2tog *insert hook into next st and draw up a loop; rep from * once, yarn over, draw through all 3 loops on hook.

Ss slip stitch

St(s) stitch(es)

SIZE

Approx height: 9in (23cm)

DR DEATH

Scalpels and syringes are child's play for this doctor: his tools of the trade are specially sharpened scalpels and axes and for him the only good patient is a dead one. He greets you with a smile, but his bedside manner will have you out of bed and running if you value your life.

SHOES & LEGS

Right shoe & leg:

Using A, make 6ch.

Round 1: 2sc in second ch from hook. 1sc in each of next 3ch, 3sc in last ch. Working on other side of chain, 1sc in each of next 3ch, 2sc in last ch. (14 sts)

Cont working in back of loops only.

Round 2: 1sc in each st. (14 sts)

Round 3: 1sc in each of next 4 sts, sc2tog twice, 1sc in each of last 6 sts. (12 sts)

Round 4: 1sc in each of next 3 sts, sc2tog, 1sc, sc2tog, 1sc in each of last 4 sts. (10 sts)

Round 5: 1sc in each of next 2 sts, sc2tog, 1sc, sc2tog, 1sc in each of last 3 sts. (8 sts)

Begin working in both loops.

Rounds 6–9: 1sc in each st. (8 sts)

Change to B, begin working in back loops only.

Round 10: 1sc in each st. (8 sts)

Round 11: [1sc in each of next 2 sts, 2sc in next st] twice, 1sc in each of last 2 sts. (10 sts)

Begin working in both loops.

Rounds 12–17: 1sc in each st.

Fasten off.

Left shoe & leg:

Rep first shoe and leg. Do not fasten off before stuffing.

Stuff legs. Pin legs together with long quilting pins, so both feet are facing in same direction.

Body:

Cont using B, insert hook into unfastened-off st on second leg. Mark beg of round into first st with st marker.

Round 1: 1sc in each of next 5 sts around leg toward back. Insert hook into corresponding st of other leg. Join legs tog by making 1sc in each of next 10 sts of first leg, 1sc into each of next 5 sts of second leg. (20 sts)

Rounds 2–13: 1sc in each st. (20 sts)

Round 14: *1sc, sc2tog; rep from * to last 2 sts, 1sc in each st. (14 sts)

Round 15: Rep Round 14. (10 sts)

Stuff body.

Do not fasten off.

Head:

Cont using B.

Round 1: 1sc in each st. (10 sts)

Round 2: *1sc in next st, 2sc in next st; rep from * to end of round. (15 sts)

Round 3: *1sc in each of next 2 sts, 2sc in next st; rep from * to end of round. (20 sts)

Round 4: *1sc in each of next 3 sts, 2sc in next st; rep from * to end of round. (25 sts)

Rounds 5–9: 1sc in each st. (25 sts)

Round 10: *1sc in next st, sc2tog; rep from * to end of round. (17 sts)

Cut small felt circles, cut slits in center and insert safety eyes. Insert eyes into face. Stuff head.

Round 11: *1sc in next st, sc2tog; rep from * to last 2 sts, sc2tog. (11 sts)

Round 12: Sc2tog around.

Fasten off.

ARMS (make 2)

Using B, make 2ch, 5sc in second ch from hook.

Round 1: *1sc in next st, 2sc in next st; rep from * once, 1sc in last st. (7 sts)

Rounds 2–4: 1sc in each st.

Next row: 1sc in each st until arm measures 3½in (9cm).

Fasten off.

MAKING UP

Stuff arms, pin and sew to body.

Sew felt circles onto face. Embroider eyebrows using C.

MASK

Make a small hem on all four sides of fabric. Make a stitch with embroidery floss into each corner, leaving a length of floss long enough to tie a bow at back of head. Hand sew mask onto face down two sides and bottom of mask, leaving top open. Insert a small amount of stuffing into top. Tie mask ties at back.

SCRUBS

Top:

Step 1: Fold cotton fabric and using the template on page 108 with shoulders to the folded edge, cut out scrubs top.

Step 2: Make a small hem on the sleeves and bottom.

Step 3: Hand sew in blanket stitch around the neckline.

Step 4: Sew sleeve and side seams. Turn right side out and put on doll.

Pants:

Step 1: Fold cotton fabric and using the template on page 108 with straight edge of pants at folded edge, cut out 2 pieces for pants.

Step 2: Open each piece out and put wrong side together matching up edges. Sew seam down each curved edge.

Step 3: Open out with seams at front and back. Match up legs and sew down each leg seam.

Step 4: Sew hems.

Step 5: Turn right side out. Fit pants onto doll and hand stitch around waist to secure.

Smear red acrylic paint over scrubs and mask and insert tools into doll hands.

HAIR

Cut approx 30 strands of C, each 3in (7.5cm) long. Fold each strand of yarn in half one at a time and loop strands into stitches on head around the crown. Trim as necessary to give doll a wild look.

PIERCING PHYLLIS

Phyllis is one of the most scary of all the scaries—she has no stop button and always takes things too far. She likes to be well dressed; she polishes and shines the spikes on her pins, but when someone upsets her she pulls the pins out of her head and stabs them. She has recently taken up dancing Modern Jive.

Warning: This pattern is for a toy with sharp pins. Do not use pins if giving to children and take care when handling.

MATERIALS

Pure wool light worsted (DK) yarn:
Head, Body, Legs, Hands: ½ × 1¾oz (50g) ball—approx 68.5yd (62.5m)—of beige (A)
Shoes: Small amount of black (B)
Arms: Small amount of white (C)
Fiberfill stuffing
Eye surround: Red felt
Eyes: 2 × blue flat-back beads
Mouth: Black embroidery floss
Hair, Nails: Approx 25 glass-headed pins
Vest: Small piece of black felt
Skirt: Four pieces of black netting each 14 × 3in (35 × 7.5cm)
Thin black elastic
Crochet hook size: F/5 (4mm)

ABBREVIATIONS

Ch chain
Rep repeat
Sc single crochet
Sc2tog *insert hook into next st and draw up a loop; rep from * once, yarn over, draw through all 3 loops on hook.
Ss slip stitch
St(s) stitch(es)

SIZE

Approx height: 8in (21cm)

HEAD

Using A, make 2ch, 6sc in second ch from hook.
Round 1: 2sc in each st. (12 sts)
Round 2: *1sc in next st, 2sc in next st; rep from * to end of round. (18 sts)
Round 3: *1sc in each of next 2 sts, 2sc in next st; rep from * to end of round. (24 sts)
Rounds 4–6: 1sc in each st.
Round 7: 1sc in each of next 2 sts, sc2tog; rep from * to end of round. (18 sts)
Round 8: *1sc in next st, sc2tog; rep from * to end of round. (12 sts)
Stuff head.
Round 9: Sc2tog around until opening is closed.
Fasten off.

BODY

Using A, make 2ch, 6sc in second ch from hook.
Round 1: 2sc in each st. (12 sts)
Round 2: *1sc in next st, 2sc in next st; rep from * to end of round. (18 sts)
Rounds 3–11: 1sc in each st.
Stuff body lightly.
Round 12: *1sc in next st, sc2tog; rep from * to end of round. (12 sts)
Round 13: Sc2tog around until opening is closed.
Fasten off.

SHOES & LEGS (make 2)

Using B, make 2ch, 5sc in second ch from hook.
Round 1: *1sc in next st, 2sc in next st; rep from * once, 1sc in last st. (7 sts)
Round 2: 1sc in each st.
Change to A.
Rounds 3–9: 1sc in each st.
Fasten off.

HANDS & ARMS (make 2)

Using A, make 2ch, 6sc in second ch from hook.
Round 1: *1sc in next st, 2sc in next st; rep from * to end of round. (9 sts)
Round 2: 1sc in each st.
Change to C.
Rounds 4–11: 1sc in each st.
Fasten off.

MAKING UP

Pin and sew body to head. Stuff legs and sew to body. Stuff arms and attach to body so arms are sticking out in front, pointing forward. Push two glass-headed pins into tips of hands with sharp ends pointing out. Cut small disks of red felt and sew on as eyes, stick blue eyes on top. Embroider mouth. Stick pins in head as hair.

VEST

Using the template on page 109, cut out two pieces of black felt for vest. Sew shoulder straps and sides together. Adjust as necessary.

SKIRT

Put the four pieces of netting on top of each other. Sew a channel along one length, wide enough to thread the elastic through. Thread elastic through and gather. Sew along gathers to secure in place. Tie at back and hand stitch skirt to doll to secure.

PAYNE THE GOTH GIRL

Payne (formerly known as Evalina Angelina Pretty) grew up. And that's all. Goth girl could be you, or any of your little girls—one day pretty in pink, the next moody in mauve or beastly in black. You have been warned.

MATERIALS

Pure wool light worsted (DK) yarn:

Head, Cross, Chain: ¼ x 1¾oz (50g) ball —approx 31yd (28.5m)—of white (A)

Shoes, Body, Dress, Hair: 1 x 1¾oz (50g) ball—approx 124yd (112.5m)—of black (B)

Legs, Mouth: Small amount of purple (C)

Legs: Small amount of green (D)

Knickers: Small amount of red (E)

Arms: Small amount of beige (F)

Eye surrounds: Small piece of black felt

Safety eyes

Fiberfill stuffing

Piercing: Pin

Nose/ear beads: 8 each of white and red seed beads

Hair streaks: Strands of silver lurex and green yarn.

Crochet hook size: F/5 (4mm)

ABBREVIATIONS

Alt alternate

Beg beginning

Ch chain

Cont continue

Rep repeat

Sc single crochet

Sc2tog *insert hook into next st and draw up a loop; rep from * once, yarn over, draw through all 3 loops on hook.

Ss slip stitch

St(s) stitch(es)

SIZE

Approx height: 9½in (24cm)

HEAD

Using A, make 2ch, 6sc in second ch from hook.

Round 1: 2sc in each st. (12 sts)

Round 2: *1sc in next st, 2sc in next st; rep from * to end of round. (18 sts)

Round 3: *1sc in each of next 2 sts, 2sc in next st; rep from * to end of round. (24 sts)

Rounds 4–8: 1sc in each st. (24 sts)

Round 9: *1sc in each of next 2 sts, sc2tog; rep from * to end of round. (18 sts)

Round 10: *1sc in next st, sc2tog; rep from * to end of round. (12 sts)

Cut small circles of felt, make small hole in center and insert safety eyes. Insert eyes into head. Stuff head. Hand sew felt circles in place.

Round 11: Sc2tog around until opening is closed.

Fasten off.

SHOES, LEGS & BODY

Right shoe & leg:

Using B, make 6ch.

Round 1: 2sc in second ch from hook. 1sc in each of next 3ch, 3sc in last ch. Working on other side of chain, 1sc in each of next 3ch, 2sc in last ch. (14 sts)

Cont working in back of loops only.

Round 2: 1sc in each st. (14 sts)

Round 3: 1sc in each of next 4 sts, sc2tog twice, 1sc in each of last 6 sts. (12 sts)

Round 4: 1sc in each of next 3 sts, sc2tog, 1sc, sc2tog, 1sc in each of last 4 sts. (10 sts)

Round 5: 1sc in each of next 2 sts, sc2tog, 1sc, sc2tog, 1sc in each of last 3 sts. (8 sts)

Work alt C & D every two rows from now on. Cont working in both loops.

Rounds 6–16: 1sc in each st. (8 sts)

Round 17: *1sc in each of next 2 sts, 2sc in next st; rep from * once more, 1sc in each of next 2 sts. (10 sts)

Stuff leg and sew in ends.

Fasten off.

Left shoe & leg:

Rep first shoe and leg. Do not fasten off before stuffing.

Stuff legs and pin together with long quilting pins, so both feet are facing in same direction.

Knickers:

Using E, insert hook into unfastened-off st on left leg. Mark beg of round into first st with st marker.

Round 1: 1sc in each of next 5 sts around leg towards back. Insert hook into corresponding st of other leg. Join legs by making 1sc in each of next 10 sts of first leg, 1sc into each of next 5 sts of second leg. (20 sts)

Rounds 2–5: 1sc in each st. (20 sts)

Do not fasten off.

Body:

Change to B.

Rounds 6–13: 1sc in each st. (20 sts)

Round 14: *1sc, sc2tog; rep from * to last 2 sts, 1sc in each st. (14 sts)

Round 15: Rep Round 14. (10 sts)

Stuff body.

Round 16: Sc2tog around until opening is closed.

Fasten off.

ARMS (make 2)

Using F, make 2ch, 5sc in second ch from hook.

Round 1: *1sc in next st, 2sc in next st; rep from * once, 1sc in last st. (7 sts)

Round 2: 1sc in each st. (7 sts)

Cont working 1sc in each st until arm measures approx 3¼in (8cm).

Fasten off.

MAKING UP

Stuff arms lightly, pin and sew to body. Sew head to body. Using C, embroider mouth. Insert pin in mouth. Using a short length of white yarn, thread beads in alternating colors. Sew in place from ear area to nose area.

DRESS

Using B, make 26ch, ss into first ch to form
a ring.

Rounds 1–7: 1sc in each st. (26 sts)

Round 8: Sc2tog, 1sc in each of next 12 sts,
sc2tog, 1sc in each st to end. (24 sts)

Round 9: Sc2tog, 1sc in each of next 11 sts,
sc2tog, 1sc in each st to end. (22 sts)

Rounds 10–11: 1sc in each st. (22 sts)

Round 12: Sc2tog, 1sc in each of next 10 sts,
sc2tog, 1sc in each st to end. (20 sts)

Fasten off.

First shoulder:

With fasten-off st facing to your right, join yarn
into third st in towards center.

Row 1: 1sc in each of next 3 sts. (3 sts)

Row 2: 1sc in each of next 2 sts. (2 sts)

Row 3: Sc2tog. (1 st)

Row 4: 2ch, 2sc in second ch from hook.
(2 sts)

Row 5: 1sc in each of next 2 sts. (2 sts)

Row 6: 1sc in next st, 2sc in next st. (3 sts)

Do not fasten off.

Sleeve:

Work 10sc around straight armhole edge, ss
in first sc.

Rounds 1–8: 1sc in each st. (10 sts)

Round 9: 2sc in next st, 1sc in each st to end.
(11 sts)

Rounds 10–12: Rep Round 9. (14 sts)

Fasten off.

Second shoulder & sleeve:

With fasten-off st facing to your right, skip 1 st
and join in yarn.

Next row: Ss in each st. (3 sts)

Rep first shoulder and sleeve from Row 1,
working first 3 sts towards center.

Fit dress onto doll and sew back of shoulders
and sleeves in place.

CROSS NECKLACE

Vertical piece:

Using A, make 8ch.

Row 1: Ss into each ch.

Fasten off, sew in ends.

Horizontal piece:

Using A, make 6ch.

Row 1: Ss into each ch.

Fasten off, sew in ends.

Place horizontal piece on top of vertical piece
and sew in place.

CHAIN

Using A, join yarn into top of cross. Make 25ch,
join necklace with a ss into top of cross (in
same space as the start).

Fasten off, sew in ends.

Attach necklace round doll's neck.

HAIR

Using B, cut several strands of yarn each approx
4in (10cm) long. Loop each strand all around
head. Attach one piece of green and one piece
of silver Lurex into hair.

FRANKENSTEIN'S YOUNGSTER

The Youngster has a scar on his face from doing something silly while on a snowboarding holiday. In everyday life he dresses casually and inserts a clean bolt through his neck daily. He is always hoping to meet a nice girl to go out with, but so far has been unlucky, as he scares everyone he meets.

MATERIALS

Pure wool light worsted (DK) yarn:

Shoes: Small amount of light brown (A)

Pants, Hair: ½ × 1¾oz (50g) ball—approx 62yd (56.5m)—of brown (B)

Body: ¼ × 1¾oz (50g) ball—approx 31yd (28.5m)—of gray (C)

Head, Arms: ½ × 1¾oz (50g) ball—approx 62yd (56.5m)—of beige (D)

Hair: ½ × 1¾oz (50g) ball—approx 62yd (56.5m)—of dark brown (E)

Eye surrounds: Small piece of green felt

Safety eyes

Fiberfill stuffing

Eyebrows, Mouth: Black yarn

Scar: Red embroidery floss

Jacket: Small amount check cotton fabric

Nut and bolt

Crochet hook size: F/5 (4mm)

ABBREVIATIONS

Beg beginning

Ch chain

Cont continue

Rep repeat

Sc single crochet

Sc2tog *insert hook into next st and draw up a loop; rep from * once, yarn over, draw through all 3 loops on hook.

Ss slip stitch

St(s) stitch(es)

SIZE

Approx height: 9¾in (25cm)

SHOES, LEGS & BODY

Right shoe & leg:

Using A, make 6ch.

Round 1: 2sc in second ch from hook. 1sc in each of next 3ch, 3sc in last ch. Working on other side of ch, 1sc in each of next 3ch, 2sc in last ch. (14 sts)

Cont working in back of loops only.

Round 2: 1sc in each st. (14 sts)

Round 3: 1sc in each of next 4 sts, sc2tog twice, 1sc in each of last 6 sts. (12 sts)

Change to B, cont working in both loops.

Round 4: 1sc in each of next 3 sts, sc2tog, 1sc, sc2tog, 1sc in each of last 4 sts. (10 sts)

Round 5: 1sc in each of next 2 sts, sc2tog, 1sc, sc2tog, 1sc in each of last 3 sts. (8 sts)

Rounds 6–10: 1sc in each st. (8 sts)

Round 11: *1sc in each of next 2 sts, 2sc in next st; rep from * to last 2 sts, 1sc in each st. (10 sts)

Rounds 12–17: 1sc in each st. (10 sts)

Fasten off.

Left shoe & leg:

Rep first shoe and leg. Do not fasten off before stuffing.

Stuff legs and pin together with long quilting pins, so that both feet are facing in the same direction.

Body:

Using B, make 1sc in each of next 5 sts around second leg. Mark beg of round into first st with st marker.

Round 1: Insert hook into middle st at back of leg. Join legs together by making 1sc in each of next 10 sts of first leg, 1sc into each of next 5 sts of second leg. (20 sts)

Rounds 2–4: 1sc in each st. (20 sts)

Change to C.

Rounds 5–12: 1sc in each st.

Round 13: *1sc in next st, sc2tog; rep from * to last 2 sts, 1sc in each st. (14 sts)

Round 14: *1sc in next st, sc2tog; rep from * to last 2 sts, 1sc in each st. (10 sts)

Stuff body.

Round 15: Sc2tog around until opening is closed.

Fasten off.

HEAD

Starting at top of head and using D, make 2ch, 6sc in second ch from hook.

Round 1: 2sc in each st. (12 sts)

Round 2: *1sc in next st, 2sc in next st; rep from * to end of round. (18 sts)

Round 3: *1sc in each of next 2 sts, 2sc in next st; rep from * to end of round. (24 sts)

Rounds 4–8: 1sc in each st. (24 sts)

Round 9: *1sc in each of next 2 sts, sc2tog; rep from * to end of round. (18 sts)

Round 10: *1sc in next st, sc2tog; rep from * to end of round. (12 sts)

Cut two small felt circles, make a hole in the center of each and insert safety eyes. Insert eyes into face. Hand sew felt circles to head. Stuff head carefully, placing most of stuffing to bottom and very little at top.

Round 11: 1sc in each st. (12 sts)

Round 12: Sc2tog until opening is closed. Fasten off.

ARMS (make 2)

Using D, make 2ch, 5sc in second ch from hook.

Round 1: *2sc in next st, 1sc in next st; rep from * once, 2sc in last st. (8 sts)

Rounds 2–11: 1sc in each st. (8 sts) Fasten off.

MAKING UP

Sew in ends, keeping top of head flat. Pin and sew head to body. Embroider mouth and eyebrows. Embroider scar. Stuff arms lightly and attach to body. Thread bolt through neck and add nut.

JACKET

The exact size of jacket will depend on finished size of doll. Use the template on page 109 as a guide, but adjust sizing as necessary. Using the template, cut two pieces of fabric. Cut one in half for the front pieces. With wrong sides together, sew back to front along arm, side, and shoulder seams. Cut a 1in (2.5cm) wide strip of fabric to fit round right front, back, and left front. Make a hem down each front. Fold each side into center lengthwise. Press and fold in half. Attach to shirt around neck to make a collar. Roll up sleeves.

HAIR

Thread a tapestry needle with E and embroider a fringe and hair to back of head. Cut six strands of B and make a braid approx 2in (5cm) long. Sew braid onto back of head.

NOBBY THE DEAD ROCKER

Nobby Nosebleed was just an ordinary rock star until he was bitten by a bat onstage and died—which did wonders for his flagging career. His latest smash hit is "Don't Go Breaking My Heart (Because It's In Quite A Valuable Jar Somewhere)."

MATERIALS

Pure wool light worsted (DK) yarn:
Shoes: Small amount of dark red (A)
Legs, Body, Arms, Sunglasses, Hair:
   1½ x 1¾oz (50g) balls—approx 185yd
   (169m)—of black (B)
Head, Hands: ¼ x 1¾oz (50g) ball
   —approx 34.5yd (31.5m)—of
   off-white (C)
Mouth: Small amount of bright red
Fiberfill stuffing
Bling: Approx 10in (25cm) string of beads
   and coins
Crochet hook size: E/4 (3.5mm)

ABBREVIATIONS

Beg beginning
Ch chain
Cont continue
Rep repeat
Sc single crochet
Sc2tog *insert hook into next st and draw
   up a loop; rep from * once, yarn over;
   draw through all 3 loops on hook.
Ss slip stitch
St(s) stitch(es)
Tog together

SIZE

Approx height: 10in (25.5cm)

SHOES, LEGS, BODY & HEAD

Right shoe & leg:
Using A, make 6ch.
Round 1: 2sc in second ch from hook. 1sc in each of next 3ch, 3sc in last ch. Working on other side of chain, 1sc in each of next 3ch, 2sc in last ch. (14 sts)
Insert st marker in loop on hook. Cont working in back of loops only.
Round 2: 1sc in each st. (14 sts)
Round 3: 1sc in each of next 4 sts, sc2tog twice, 1sc in each of last 6 sts. (12 sts)
Round 4: 1sc in each of next 3 sts, sc2tog, 1sc, sc2tog, 1sc in each of last 4 sts. (10 sts)
Round 5: 1sc in each of next 2 sts, sc2tog, 1sc, sc2tog, 1sc in each of last 3 sts. (8 sts)
Change to B and begin working in both loops.
Rounds 6–10: 1sc in each st. (8 sts)
Round 11: [1sc in each of next 2 sts, 2sc in next st] twice, 1sc in each of last 2 sts. (10 sts)
Rounds 12–17: 1sc in each st.
Fasten off.

Left shoe & leg:
Rep first shoe and leg. Do not fasten off before stuffing.
Stuff legs. Pin legs together with long quilting pins, so both feet are facing in same direction.

Body:
Cont using B, insert hook into unfastened-off st on second leg. Mark beg of round into first st with st marker.
Round 1: 1sc in each of next 5 sts around leg toward back. Insert hook into corresponding st of other leg. Join legs tog by making 1sc in each of next 10 sts of first leg, 1sc into each of next 5 sts of second leg. (20 sts)
Rounds 2–13: 1sc in each st. (20 sts)
Round 14: *1sc, sc2tog; rep from * to last 2 sts, 1sc in each st. (14 sts)
Round 15: Rep Round 14. (10 sts)
Stuff body.
Do not fasten off.

Head:
Join in C.
Round 1: 1sc in each st. (10 sts)
Round 2: *1sc in next st, 2sc in next st; rep from * to end of round. (15 sts)
Round 3: *1sc in each of next 2 sts, 2sc in next st; rep from * to end of round. (20 sts)
Round 4: *1sc in each of next 3 sts, 2sc in next st; rep from * to end of round. (25 sts)
Rounds 5–9: 1sc in each st. (25 sts)
Round 10: *1sc in next st, sc2tog; rep from * to end of round. (17 sts)
Stuff head.
Round 11: *1sc in next st, sc2tog; rep from * to last 2 sts, sc2tog. (11 sts)
Round 12: Sc2tog around.
Fasten off.

HANDS & ARMS (make 2)

Using C, make 2ch, 5sc in second ch from hook.

Round 1: *1sc in next st, 2sc in next st; rep from * once, 1sc in last st. (7 sts)

Rounds 2–4: 1sc in each st. (7 sts)

Change to B.

Next row: 1sc in each st until arm measures 3½in (9cm).

Fasten off.

MAKING UP

Do not stuff arms, pin and sew to body. Sew mouth using bright red yarn. Using B, embroider sunglasses onto doll's face.

HAIR

Cut approx 140 strands of B each measuring 8in (20cm). Place strands across head evenly and spread gently toward back. Make back stitches from forehead to back of head creating a center parting. Make small stitches around crown to secure hair in place.

BLING

Attach bling in place around neck and hips and sew in place with cotton thread.

MATERIALS

ALL TOMATOES

Wool worsted (Aran) yarn:

½ × 1¾oz (50g) ball—approx 51.5yd (47m)—of red (A)

½ × 1¾oz (50g) ball—approx 51.5yd (47m)—of yellow (B)

1 × 1¾oz (50g) ball—approx 103yd (94m)—of green (C)

Pair safety eyes for each

Fiberfill stuffing

Crochet hook size: F/5 (4mm)

BEEF-I-AM

Mouth: Black yarn

Teeth: 7 tooth shape beads decorated with gold nail varnish or gold pen

CHERRY

Eyebrows: Black yarn

Mouth: Red yarn

Small safety pin

Gold/brass hoop earrings, approx 1in (2.5cm) diameter

CHUTNEY

Eyebrows, Mouth: Black yarn

Bandana: Triangular piece of fabric, approx width 19½in (49.5cm), point to straight edge 5in (12.5cm)

ABBREVIATIONS

Ch chain

Cont continue

Rep repeat

Sc single crochet

Sc2tog *insert hook into next st and draw up a loop; rep from * once, yarn over, draw through all 3 loops on hook.

Ss slip stitch

St(s) stitch(es)

SIZE

Approx height: 8in (20cm)

TOMATOES FROM THE 'HOOD

The Tomatoes are Beef-i-am (red), Cherry (yellow), and Chutney (green). They hang around the vine intimidating other vegetables—no one dares mess with them. They prowl the 'hood looking for action, and if there's trouble around it's hot tomato salsa!

TOMATOES (make 1 in each color)

Using A, B, or C make 2ch, 6sc in second ch from hook.

Round 1: 2sc in each st. (12 sts)

Round 2: *1sc in next st, 2sc in next st; rep from * to end of round. (18 sts)

Round 3: *1sc in each of next 2 sts, 2sc in next st; rep from * to end of round. (24 sts)

Round 4: 1sc in each st. (24 sts)

Round 5: *1sc in each of next 3 sts, 2sc in next st; rep from * to end. (30 sts)

Round 6: 1sc in each st.

Round 7: *1sc in each of next 4 sts, sc2tog; rep from * to end of round. (25 sts)

Round 8: 1sc in each st. (25 sts)

Round 9: *1sc in each of next 3 sts, sc2tog; rep from * to end of round. (20 sts)

Round 10: 1sc in each st. (20 sts)

Insert safety eyes.

Red and yellow tomatoes only: change to C.

Round 11: *1sc in each of next 2 sts, sc2tog; rep from * to end. (15 sts)

Stuff.

Round 12: *1sc in next st, sc2tog; rep from * to end of round. (10 sts)

Round 13: Sc2tog 5 times. (5 sts)

Fasten off, leaving a long tail.

Stalk for red and yellow tomatoes:

Thread long end of yarn into tapestry needle and draw yarn through final 5 sts tightly.

Insert hook into center and using yarn end, make 5ch, ss into second ch from hook and each of the following ch, ss into base of original ch.

Fasten off.

LEAVES

Red and yellow tomatoes only, join C into any loop from Round 12, make 3ch, ss back into joining st, *ss into each of next 2 loops, 3ch, ss back into base of last ss; rep from * around.

Join with a ss into first loop.

Fasten off.

MAKING UP

Beef-i-am:

Embroider mouth. Sew teeth beads in place below mouth.

Cherry:

Embroider eyebrows in black yarn and mouth in red yarn. Attach ear loops and safety pin.

Chutney:

Embroider eyebrows and mouth in black yarn. Cut triangular piece of fabric to size to fit round head with ties and hem if necessary. Tie bandana around head and hand stitch to hold in place.

CHAPTER 5
CREEPY TRINKETS

The spider's web has been spun by Cynthia, who is disguised as a bag; watch out for when she opens her mouth, a thousand flies will surround you. Wear Willy the Wolf around your neck at your peril; he has very large teeth and has also been known to bite people. Try on the Las Vegas Cross for fun or keep unwanted visitors away with the help of Shaun the Shrunken Head.

SPIDER WEB BUNTING

Made by women spiders from the forest of Radlett, who weave webs as they dance to eerie, blood-curdling grooves. When the party is over, all that remains are a few scuff marks on the floor and lovely spider webs draped everywhere.

MATERIALS

Wool/silk/cashmere laceweight yarn:
Spider web, Chains: 1 × 3½oz (100g) ball —approx 1312yd (1200m)—of white (A)
Mohair/silk laceweight yarn:
Spider web: 4 × 25g (⅞oz) balls—approx 919yd (840m)—of cream (B)
Crochet hook size: B/1 (2mm)

ABBREVIATIONS

Ch chain
Dc double crochet
Rep repeat
Sc single crochet
Sc2tog *insert hook into next st and draw up a loop; rep from * once, yarn over, draw through all 3 loops on hook.
Ss slip stitch
St(s) stitch(es)
Tr treble crochet

SIZE

Approx web diameter: 12in (30cm)
Approx chain length: 8in (20cm)

TIPS

Chains are not included in stitch counts. The webs are made using two different yarns; the mohair/silk mix gives a 'hazy' effect and the wool/silk/cashmere yarn a finer silk web. Use one for each alternate web, or just one yarn throughout.

SPIDER WEB

Using either A or B, make 8ch, join with ss to form a ring.
Round 1: 2ch, 1sc in second ch from hook, 2ch, *1dc in ring, 2ch; rep from * 6 times more, join with ss in top of first sc. (8 sts)
Round 2: 2ch, 1sc in second ch from hook, 4ch, *1dc in next st, 4ch; rep from * 6 times more, join with ss in top of first sc.
Round 3: 2ch, 1sc in second ch from hook, 6ch, *1dc in next st, 6ch; rep from * 6 times more, join with ss in top of first sc.
Round 4: 2ch, 1sc in second ch from hook, 8ch, *1dc in next st, 8ch; rep from * 6 times more, join with ss in top of first sc.
Round 5: 2ch, 1sc in second ch from hook, 10ch, *1dc in next st, 10ch; rep from * 6 times more, join with ss in top of first sc.
Round 6: 2ch, 1sc in second ch from hook, 6ch, 1sc in next 10-ch sp, 6ch, *1dc in next st, 6ch, 1sc in next 10-ch sp, 6ch; rep from * to end, join with ss in top of first sc. (16 sts)
Round 7: 2ch, 1sc in second ch from hook, 4ch, 1dc in same st as join, (this counts as 1dc, 4ch, 1dc). 4ch, [1dc, 4ch, 1dc] in next st, 4ch, *[1dc, 4ch, 1dc] in next st, 4ch [1dc, 4ch, 1dc] in next st, 4ch; rep from * to end, join with ss in top of first sc. (32 sts)
Round 8: Ss into center of next 4ch sp, 2ch, 1sc in second ch from hook, 7ch, skip next 4-ch sp, *1dc in next 4-ch sp, 7ch, skip next 4-ch sp; rep from * to end, join with ss in top of first sc. (16 sts)
Round 9: 2ch, 1sc in second ch from hook, 9ch, *1dc in next st, 9ch; rep from * to end, join with ss in top of first sc.
Round 10: 2ch, 1sc in second ch from hook, 3ch, [1dc, 4ch, 1dc] in fifth ch of next 9ch sp, 3ch, *1dc in next st, 3ch, [1dc, 4ch, 1dc] in fifth ch of next 9ch sp, 3ch; rep from * to end, join with ss in top of first sc. (48 sts)
Round 11: 2ch, 1sc in second ch from hook, 2ch, 1dc in next st, 7ch, 1dc in next st, 2ch, *1dc in next st, 2ch, 1dc in next st, 7ch, 1dc in next st, 2ch; rep from * to end, join with ss in top of first sc.
Round 12: 9ch (counts as 1tr, 6ch), skip next st, 1dc in next 7-ch sp, 6ch, *skip next st, 1tr in next st, 6ch, skip next st, 1dc in next 7ch sp, 6ch; rep from * to end, join with ss in third of first 9-ch. (32 sts)
Round 13: 2ch, 1sc in second ch from hook, 7ch, 1dc in next st, 7ch, *1dc in next st, 7ch, 1dc in next st 7ch; rep from * to end, join with ss in top of first sc.
Fasten off.

MAKING UP

Make two chains to join each spider web to the next and add two chains at each end as ties.

Chains:
Using A, make 40ch.
Fasten off.
Rep for each chain required. Join spider webs using yarn ends of chains.

WILLY THE WILY WOLF

Willy the Wily Wolf loves to hang out... around necks. He lies around looking cute and fluffy and people love to wrap up in him. Then he strikes; he bites quickly and sharply and then snuggles back against their necks, looking so innocent that nobody ever suspects him.

MATERIALS

Acrylic and mohair chunky fringed yarn:
Head, Body, Ears: 3 x 3½oz (100g) hanks —approx 118yd (108m)—of gray (A)
Pure wool light worsted (DK) yarn:
Legs: 1 x 3½oz (100g) hank—approx 218yd (200m)—of black (B)
18mm amber safety eyes
Fiberfill stuffing
Crochet hook size: P/19 (15mm), F/5 (4mm) and H/8 (5mm)

ABBREVIATIONS

Beg beginning
Ch chain
Cont continue
Foll following
Rep repeat
Sc single crochet
Sc2tog *insert hook into next st and draw up a loop; rep from * once, yarn over, draw through all 3 loops on hook.
Ss slip stitch
St(s) stitch(es)

SIZE

Approx length: 44in (112cm)
Approx width: 6in (15cm)

TIP

The stitches are difficult to see in this fluffy yarn, but the head and body are crocheted using a large hook, so the spaces are easy to feel and the stitch is found easily.

HEAD & BODY

Using P/19 (15mm) hook and A, make 2ch, turn.
Row 1: 3sc in second ch from hook.
Row 2: 1ch, 2sc in first st, 1sc in each st to last st, 2sc in last st. (5 sts)
Row 3: 1ch, 1sc in each st. (5 sts)
Row 4: 1ch, 2sc in first st, 1sc in each st to last st, 2sc in last st. (7 sts)
Row 5: 1ch, 1sc in each st. (7 sts)
Row 6: 1ch, 2sc in first st, 1sc in each st to last st, 2sc in last st. (9 sts)
Row 7: 1ch, 1sc in each st. (9 sts)
Rep Row 7 until work measures 36in (91.5cm).
Next row: 1ch, skip first st, 1sc in each of foll 6 sts, skip next st, 1sc in last st. (7 sts)
Next row: 1ch, 1sc in each of foll 7 sts. (7 sts)
Next row: 1ch, skip first st, 1sc in each of next 5 sts, skip next st, 1sc in last st. (6 sts)
Next row: 1ch, 1sc in each st. (6 sts)
Rep previous row three more times.
Next row: 1ch, skip first st, 2sc in next st, skip next st, 1sc in last st. (3 sts)
Next row: 1ch, 1sc in each st. (3 sts)
Rep previous row once more.
Next row: 1ch, skip first st, 1sc in next st, ss in last st.
Fasten off.

LEGS (make 4)

Using F/5 (4mm) hook and B, make 6ch, 2sc in second ch from hook. Mark beg of round with st marker in first st.
Round 1: 2sc in each st. (12 sts)
Rounds 2–3: 1sc in each st. (12 sts)
Round 4: *1sc in first st, sc2tog in next st; rep from * to end of round. (8 sts)
Next round: 1sc in each st until leg measures 4in (10cm).
Fasten off.

EARS (make 2)

Using H/8 (5mm) hook and A, make 3ch.
Row 1: 1sc in next ch from hook, 1sc in next ch. (2 sts)
Row 2: 1sc in each of next 2 sts. (2 sts)
Row 3: Sc2tog.
Fasten off.

MAKING UP

Insert eyes in head and stuff head and body lightly. Stuff legs and sew onto body. Sew ears onto head.

CYNTHIA THE SPIDER BAG

Cynthia the Spider loves to be helpful. She can hold all your girlie goodies, although you can see from her face that she sometimes looks inside for lovely lipsticks. Keep her away from flies—they stick to her lip gloss and make a horrid mess.

MATERIALS

Pure wool light worsted (DK) yarn:
Head, Pupils, Legs, Strap: 2 x 3½oz (100g) balls—approx 440yd (402m)—of black (A)
Eyeballs, Teeth: Small amount of cream (B)
Lips: Small amount of red (C)
Purse lining: Approx 12in (30cm) cotton fabric
4in (10cm) zipper
Fiberfill stuffing
Crochet hook size: E/4 (3.5mm), F/5 (4mm) and H/8 (5mm)

ABBREVIATIONS

Beg beginning
Ch chain
Rep repeat
RS right side
Sc single crochet
Sc2tog *insert hook into next st and draw up a loop; rep from * once, yarn over, draw through all 3 loops on hook.
Ss slip stitch
St(s) stitch(es)
WS wrong side

SIZE

Approx diameter: 6in (15cm)
Approx chain length: 30in (76cm)

BACK OF HEAD

Using F/5 (4mm) hook and A, make 2ch, 6sc in second ch from hook. Place st marker at beg of each round (loop on hook counts as one st).
Round 1: 2sc in each st. (12 sts)
Round 2: *1sc in next st, 2sc in next st; rep from * to end of round. (18 sts)
Round 3: *1sc in each of next 2 sts, 2sc in next st; rep from * to end of round. (24 sts)
Round 4: *1sc in each of next 3 sts, 2sc in next st; rep from * to end of round. (30 sts)
Round 5: *1sc in each of next 4 sts, 2sc in next st; rep from * to end of round. (36 sts)
Round 6: *1sc in each of next 5 sts, 2sc in next st; rep from * to end of round. (42 sts)
Round 7: *1sc in each of next 6 sts, 2sc in next st; rep from * to end of round. (48 sts)
Round 8: *1sc in each of next 7 sts, 2sc in next st; rep from * to end of round. (54 sts)
Round 9: *1sc in each of next 8 sts, 2sc in next st; rep from * to end of round. (60 sts)
Round 10: *1sc in each of next 9 sts, 2sc in next st; rep from * to end of round. (66 sts)
Round 11: *1sc in each of next 10 sts, 2sc in next st; rep from * to end of round. (72 sts)
Round 12: 1sc in each st.
Fasten off with a long tail approx 6in (15cm).

FACE

Using F/5 (4mm) hook and A, make 2ch, 6sc in second ch from hook.
Place st marker at beg of each round (loop on hook counts as one st).
Round 1: 2sc in each st. (12 sts)
Round 2: *1sc in next st, 2sc in next st; rep from * to end of round. (18 sts)
Round 3: *1sc in each of next 2 sts, 2sc in next st; rep from * to end of round. (24 sts)
Round 4: *1sc in each of next 3 sts, 2sc in next st; rep from * to end of round. (30 sts)
Rounds 5–6: 1sc in each st.
Round 7: *1sc in each of next 4 sts, 2sc in next st; rep from * to end of round. (36 sts)
Round 8: *1sc in each of next 5 sts, 2sc in next st; rep from * to end of round. (42 sts)
Round 9: *1sc in each of next 6 sts, 2sc in next st; rep from * to end of round. (48 sts)
Round 10: *1sc in each of next 7 sts, 2sc in next st; rep from * to end of round. (54 sts)
Round 11: *1sc in each of next 8 sts, 2sc in next st; rep from * to end of round. (60 sts)
Round 12: *1sc in each of next 9 sts, 2sc in next st; rep from * to end of round. (66 sts)
Rounds 13–14: 1sc in each st.
Fasten off with a long tail approx 6in (15cm).

LINING

Step 1: Cut two circles of lining fabric same size as crocheted pieces, plus ⅝in (1.5cm) extra all round for seam allowance.
Step 2: With RS tog, measure and pin approx 6in (15cm) around, ⅝in (1.5cm) in from edge.
Step 3: Fold one side down to line of pins and press along line, making a ⅝in (1.5cm) fold. Rep on other side.
Step 4: Lift flaps and baste both sides tog along pressed seam line. Remove pins, open out seam, and press.
Step 5: Place zipper onto opened out seam and centralize with zipper pull facing downward. Put chalk mark or pin marker on fabric at each end of zipper teeth, take zipper away and mark same point on WS of flaps.

Step 6: With RS of flaps tog, sew short seam at one end of fabric from edge of pressed line to approx ¼in (0.5cm) past mark. Rep at other end.

Step 7: Remove pins before pressing. With RS face down, open seam and press. Place zip upside down on seam and centralize again. Pin and tack zip in place on WS of fabric (RS of flaps). Remove pins from fabric.

Step 8: Turn fabric over and with RS facing, take out middle seam line tacking stitches for approx ¾ of zip length at zip pull end. Open zip approx ¾ of length from zip end.

Step 9: Put zipper foot on sewing machine (if you have one). With zip side facing, sew zip around all four sides. Take out tacking stitches and open zip. Turn RS out. Sew around circle up to zip.

Step 10: Sew two crochet circles RS together leaving enough space open for zip. Turn through and pin purse lining in place inside crochet purse.

Step 11: Insert stuffing between lining and crochet face of spider, filling nose section well. Hand sew zip to crochet open edges to secure. Crochet or sew seam closed.

EYEBALLS (make 2)

Using E/4 (3.5mm) hook and B, make 2ch, 6sc in second ch from hook.
Round 1: 2sc in each st. (12 sts)
Round 2: *1sc in next st, 2sc in next st; rep from * to end of round. (18 sts)
Rounds 3–5: 1sc in each st. (18 sts)
Round 6: Sc2tog around. (9 sts)
Fasten off with a long tail approx 6in (15cm).

PUPILS (make 2)

Using E/4 (3.5mm) hook and A, make 2ch.
Round 1: 6sc in second ch from hook. Join with ss in first sc.
Fasten off leaving long end for sewing up.

LEGS (make 8)

Using E/4 (3.5mm) hook and A, make 2ch, 6sc in second ch from hook. Place st marker into loop on hook.
Round 1: *1sc in first st, 2sc in next st; rep from * to end of round. (9 sts)
Rounds 2–3: 1sc in each st (9 sts)
Round 4: *1sc in first st, sc2tog in next st: rep from * to end of round. (6 sts)
Rounds 5–17: 1sc in each st to end of round. (6 sts)
Fasten off.

MAKING UP

Sew in ends. Stuff eyeball. Thread end through tapestry needle/wool needle and weave through rem sts, then pull to close opening. Sew pupil to eyeball. Sew eyeballs close together on face with pupils slightly offset to give a cross-eyed look. Sew legs onto body.

MOUTH

Use the photo as a guide; the row of sc next to the zip is the teeth position and the next row is the position for the lips.

Lips:
Starting two rows above zip and using red yarn, start at one end and sew a row of closely packed vertical lines over sc row to end. If necessary work twice for extra thickness.

Teeth:
Using white yarn, embroider a row of triangles the length of mouth and across row of sc right next to lips. Bring needle up through bottom point of each triangle and work towards top to fill in gap of triangle with stitches.

STRAP

Measure approx 9yd (8m) of A and fold in half. Use yarn doubled throughout as follows:
Using H/8 (5mm) hook join yarn into top back of head 3 rows behind one corner of zip.
Make 100ch (or adjust length to suit). Join with a ss into top back of head 3 rows behind other corner of zip.

LAS VEGAS CROSS NECKLACE

Dress up in black as a priest or a nun and have fun with this sparkly crocheted cross. The creepy skull button and blood-red sequins make it the ideal accessory for all those aspiring Goths out there.

MATERIALS

Pure wool light worsted (DK) yarn:
Cross: ½ × 1¾oz (50g) ball—approx 55yd (50m)—of white (A)
Cord: ¼ × 1¾oz (50g) ball—approx 27.5yd (25m)—of black (B)
Fiberfill stuffing
Black and red sequins
Skull button
Crochet hook sizes: E/4 (3.5mm) and K10½ (7mm)

ABBREVIATIONS

Ch chain
Cont continue
Rep repeat
Sc single crochet
Sc2tog *insert hook into next st and draw up a loop; rep from * once, yarn over; draw through all 3 loops on hook.
Ss slip stitch
St(s) stitch(es)

SIZE

Approx height cross: 5½in (14cm)
Approx length necklace: 35½in (90cm)

VERTICAL ARM (make 1)

Using E/4 (3.5mm) hook and A, make 2ch, 8sc into second ch from hook.
Round 1: *1sc in next st, 2sc in next st; rep from * to end of round. (12 sts)
Cont working in back loops only.
Round 2: 1sc in each st to end of round. (12 sts)
Cont working in both loops.
Rounds 3–24: 1sc in each st.
Stuff lightly.
Cont working in back loops only.
Round 25: *1sc, sc2tog; rep from * to end of round. (8 sts)
Round 26: Sc2tog around. (4 sts)
Fasten off.

HORIZONTAL ARMS (make 2)

Using E/4 (3.5mm) hook and A, make 2ch, 8sc in second ch from hook
Round 1: *1sc in next st, 2sc in next st; rep from * to end of round. (12 sts)
Cont working in back loops only.
Round 2: 1sc in each st to end. (12 sts)
Cont working in both loops.
Rounds 3–7: 1sc in each st.
Stuff lightly.
Fasten off.

MAKING UP

Sew in ends. Attach two side arms to central arm positioned approx three quarters up from bottom. Hand sew sequins and skull button to decorate cross.

NECK CORD

Using B, cut 3 lengths around 160in (400cm). With K10½ (7mm) hook and using three strands together throughout, join yarn to one side of top of cross and make 80ch.
Join ch to opposite side at the top with a ss.
Fasten off.
Sew in ends.

SHAUN THE SHRUNKEN HEAD

When Shaun was in his mid-forties his head was cut off and boiled in water for half an hour to reduce it to about half its original size (he used to have a very big head). It was then placed over a stick and left to dry. His mouth was tied so he couldn't speak evil, and then there was much celebrating from the tribe who wanted to avenge his soul.

MATERIALS

Pure wool light worsted (DK) yarn:
Head: ¼ × 1¾oz (50g) ball—approx 31yd (28.5m)—of pale brown (A)
Hair: ¼ × 1¾oz (50g) ball—approx 31yd (28.5m)—of dark brown (B)
Eyebrows, Mouth, Necklace cord: ¼ × 1¾oz (50g) ball—approx 31yd (28.5m)—of black (C)
Mouth ties, Nose bone, Teeth: Small amount of white (D)
Eye surrounds: small piece of black felt
Black safety eyes
Fiberfill stuffing
3 × small red beads
1 small yellow feather
1½in (4cm) approx 30 gauge fine white floristry wire
Crochet hook size: F/5 (4mm) and C/2 (2.5mm)

ABBREVIATIONS

Ch chain
Rep repeat
Sc single crochet
Sc2tog *insert hook into next st and draw up a loop; rep from * once, yarn over, draw through all 3 loops on hook.
Ss slip stitch
St(s) stitch(es)
Tog together

SIZE

Approx head circumference: 6in (15cm)
Approx necklace length: 29in (73cm)

HEAD

Using A and F/5 (4mm) hook, 2ch, 6sc in second ch from hook.
Round 1: 2sc in each st. (12 sts)
Round 2: *1sc in next st, 2sc in next st; rep from * to end of round. (18 sts)
Rounds 3–4: 1sc in each st.
Round 5: *1sc in next st, sc2tog; rep from * to end of round. (12 sts)
Cut out two small circles in black felt slightly bigger than safety eyes. Make a slit in the center of each and insert safety eyes. Insert eyes into head. Stuff head.
Round 6: Sc2tog around until opening is closed.
Fasten off.

MAKING UP

Using C, embroider eyebrows. Hand sew felt around eyes to secure, using cotton thread.

MOUTH

Using C, embroider mouth.
Make three mouth ties one at each side of mouth and one in middle as follows:
Thread a small red bead onto a short length of D in a tapestry/wool sewing needle and make a knot to secure at the end. Sew yarn through mouth from bottom, bringing needle above mouth and over, tie a knot and push end into face to secure.
Using cotton thread, sew end of feather to bottom of middle mouth tie.

NOSE BONE

Thread piece of floristry wire through nose area. Bend each side into a loop and bend edges to create a triangular/bone shape. Cut off any excess wire.
Using D, wrap yarn round wire, completely covering it, and secure in place.

HAIR

Cut approx 40 strands of B each around 9in (23cm). Using a crochet hook, loop individual strands around hairline and round the back of head.

NECKLACE CORD

Using C double and F/5 (4mm) hook, join yarn
to top of head. Make 100ch, join with ss to
top of head.
Fasten off.
Sew in ends.

TEETH (make 20)

Using D and C/2 (2.5mm) hook, make 6ch. 1sc
into second chain from hook.
Row 1: 1sc in each ch. (5 sts)
Row 2: Skip 1 st, 1sc into each st to end. (4 sts)
Row 3: Skip 1 st, 1sc into each st to end. (3 sts)
Row 4: Skip 1 st, 1sc into each st to end. (2 sts)
Row 5: Skip 1 st, 1sc into each st to end. (1 st)
Fasten off leaving long tail of approx 6in (15cm).
Fold piece in half lengthways and using yarn tail,
sew tog starting at narrow end.
Sew in ends.
Pin teeth evenly along chain necklace. Thread
tapestry needle with a long piece of C and,
starting at bottom, stitch teeth in place using
one piece of yarn by weaving in and out of
neck chain in between attaching teeth.
Fasten off.
Sew in ends.

TECHNIQUES

HOLDING YOUR HOOK

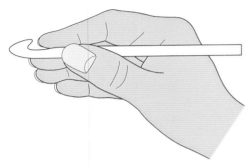

Pick up your hook as though you are picking up a pen or pencil. Keeping the hook held loosely between your fingers and thumb, turn the hook so that the tip is facing up and the hook is balanced in your hand and resting in the space between your index finger and your thumb.

HOLDING YOUR YARN

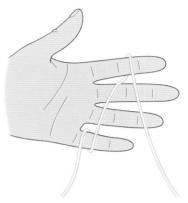

Pick up the yarn with your little finger on the opposite hand to the hook, with palm facing toward you, the short end in front of the finger and the yarn in the crease between little finger and ring finger. Turn your hand to face downward, placing the long yarn strand on top of your index finger, under the other two fingers, and wrapped right around the little finger. Then turn your hand to face you (see above), ready to hold the work in your middle finger and thumb.

YARN OVER HOOK
(yoh)

To create a stitch, catch the yarn from behind with the hook pointing upward. As you gently pull the yarn through the loop on the hook, turn the hook so it faces downward and slide the yarn through the loop. The loop on the hook should be kept loose enough for the hook to slide through easily.

MAKING A SLIP KNOT

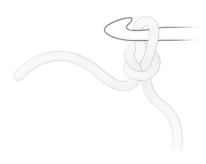

1 In one hand hold the circle at the top where the yarn crosses, and let the tail drop down at the back so that it falls across the center of the loop. With your free hand or the tip of a crochet hook, pull a loop through the circle.

2 Put the hook into the loop and pull gently so that it forms a loose loop on the hook.

CHAIN STITCHES
(ch)

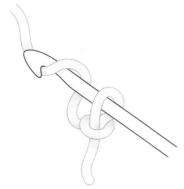

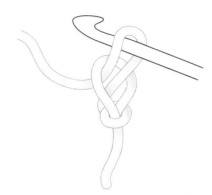

1 Using the hook, wrap the yarn over the hook ready to pull it through the loop on the hook.

2 Pull through, creating a new loop on the hook. Continue in this way to create a chain of the required length.

CHAIN SPACE
(ch sp)

1 A chain space is the space that has been made under a chain in the previous round or row, and falls in between other stitches.

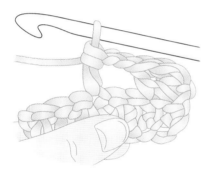

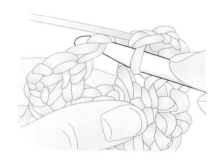

2 Stitches into a chain space are made directly into the hole created under the chain and not into the chain stitches themselves.

SLIP STITCH
(ss)

A slip stitch doesn't create any height and is often used as the last stitch to create a smooth and even round or row.

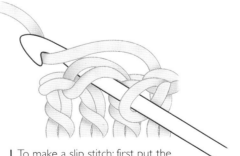

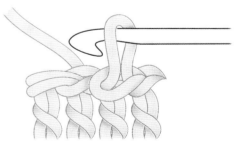

1 To make a slip stitch: first put the hook through the work, yarn over hook.

2 Pull the yarn through both the work and through the loop on the hook at the same time, so you will have 1 loop on the hook.

WORKING IN ROUNDS

There are generally two methods to working in the round: either spirals or circles.

SPIRALS

1 Spirals are started by making 2 chains and then making a group of stitches into the second chain from the hook, which creates a fan effect and is the beginning of the spiral.

2 Insert a strand of contrast yarn as a stitch marker in the loop on the hook when you have finished making the first stitches, to mark the beginning of the round. Pop the strands of the stitch marker to sit at the back of the loop—or you can use a safety pin (see opposite page). The start of the round will be made into the first stitch.

CHAIN RING/CIRCLE

If you are crocheting a round shape, one way of starting off is by crocheting a number of chains following the instructions in your pattern, and then joining them into a circle.

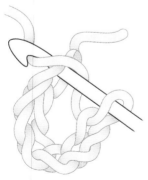

1 To join the chain into a circle, insert the crochet hook into the first chain that you made (not into the slip knot), yarn over hook.

2 Pull the yarn through the chain and through the loop on your hook at the same time, thereby creating a slip stitch and forming a circle. You now have a chain ring ready to work stitches into as instructed in the pattern.

MARKING ROUNDS

Marking rounds is an essential tool in this book. Place a stitch marker at the beginning of each round; a safety pin or piece of yarn in a contrasting color are useful for this. Loop the stitch marker into the last stitch; when you have made a round and reached the point where the stitch marker is, work this stitch, take out the stitch marker from the previous round and put it back into the loop on the hook.

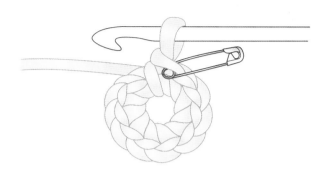

MAKING ROWS

When making straight rows you turn the work at the end of each row and make a turning chain to create the height you need for the stitch you are working with, as for making rounds. To do this, just make the right number of chains for each stitch as follows:

Single crochet = 1 chain
Half double crochet = 2 chains
Double crochet = 3 chains
Treble crochet = 4 chains

SINGLE CROCHET
(sc)

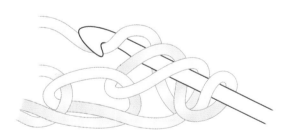

1 Insert the hook into your work, yarn over hook and pull the yarn through the work only. You will then have 2 loops on the hook.

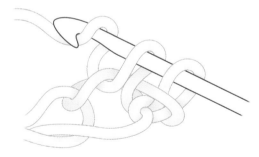

2 Yarn over hook again and pull through the two loops on the hook. You will then have 1 loop on the hook..

HALF DOUBLE CROCHET
(hdc)

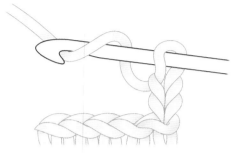 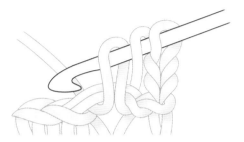 

1 Before inserting the hook into the work, wrap the yarn round the hook and put the hook through the work with the yarn wrapped around.

2 Yarn over hook again and pull through the first loop on the hook. You now have 3 loops on the hook.

3 Yarn over hook and pull the yarn through all 3 loops. You will be left with 1 loop on the hook.

DOUBLE CROCHET
(dc)

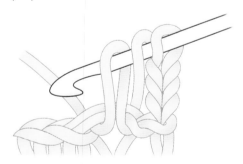  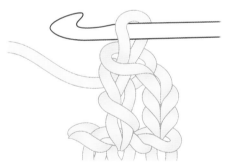

1 Before inserting the hook into the work, wrap the yarn round the hook. Put the hook through the work with the yarn wrapped around, yarn over hook again and pull through the first loop on the hook. You now have 3 loops on the hook.

2 Yarn over hook again, pull the yarn through the first 2 loops on the hook. You now have 2 loops on the hook.

3 Pull the yarn through 2 loops again. You will be left with 1 loop on the hook.

SINGLE CROCHET TWO STITCHES TOGETHER
(sc2tog)

1 Insert the hook into your work, yarn over hook and pull the yarn through the work (2 loops on hook). Insert the hook in next stitch, yarn over hook and pull the yarn through (3 loops on hook).

2 Yarn over hook again and pull through all 3 loops on the hook. You will then have 1 loop on the hook.

JOINING NEW YARN IN SINGLE CROCHET

If using single crochet to join in a new yarn, insert the hook as normal into the stitch, using the original yarn, and pull a loop through. Drop the old yarn and pick up the new yarn. Wrap the new yarn round the hook and pull it through the two loops on the hook.

WORKING INTO BACK LOOP OF STITCH

To work into the back loop of the stitch, insert the hook between the front and the back loop, picking up the back loop from the front of the work..

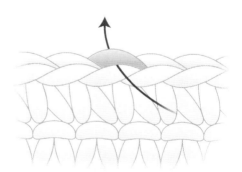

FASTENING OFF

Cut the yarn, leaving a tail of approx 15cm (6in). Pull the tail all the way through the loop.

TEMPLATES

ALIEN DAD

Page 20: Mouth and tongue

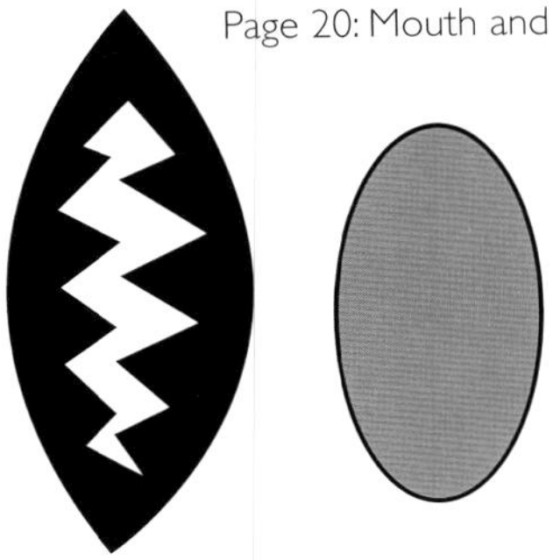

DEVIL

Page 54: Eyes and mouth

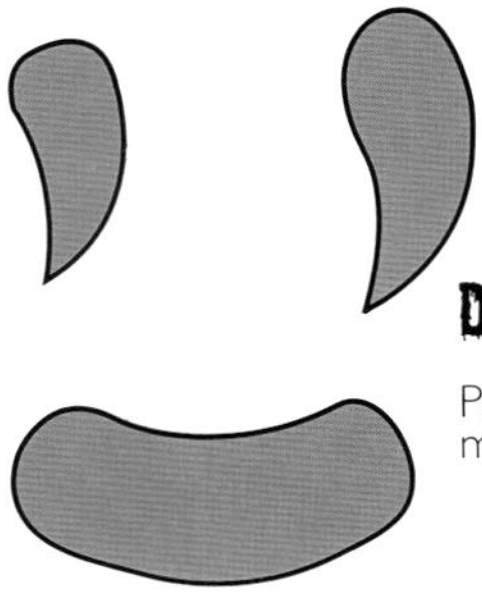

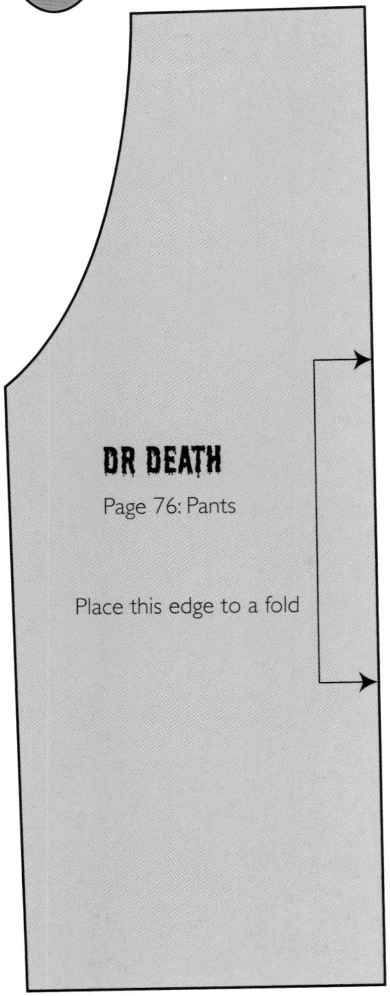

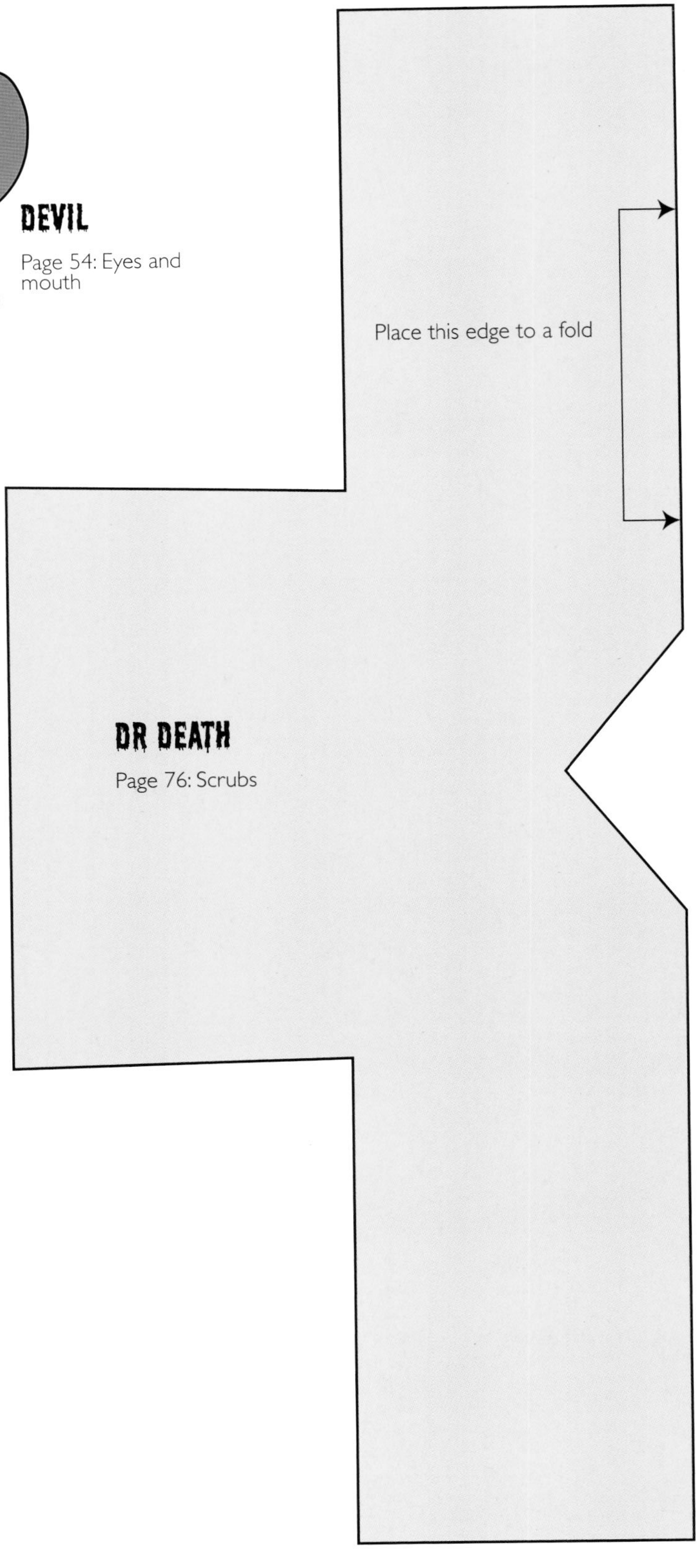

Place this edge to a fold

DR DEATH

Page 76: Scrubs

DR DEATH

Page 76: Pants

Place this edge to a fold

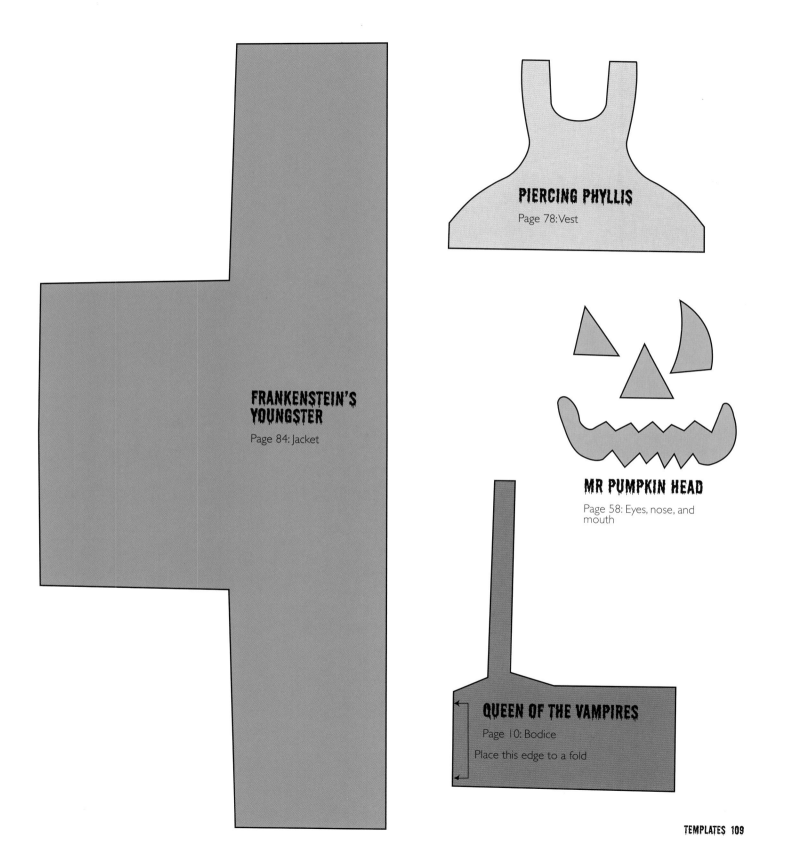

FRANKENSTEIN'S YOUNGSTER

Page 84: Jacket

PIERCING PHYLLIS

Page 78: Vest

MR PUMPKIN HEAD

Page 58: Eyes, nose, and mouth

QUEEN OF THE VAMPIRES

Page 10: Bodice

Place this edge to a fold

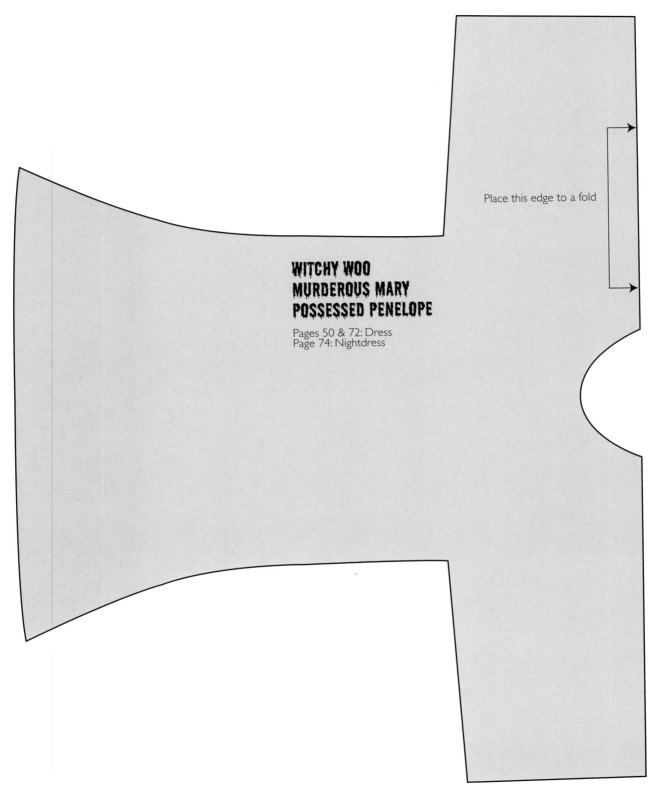

WITCHY WOO
MURDEROUS MARY
POSSESSED PENELOPE

Pages 50 & 72: Dress
Page 74: Nightdress

Place this edge to a fold

SUPPLIERS

The yarns used in these projects should be available from your local yarn or craft store. If you can't find the correct yarn, try some of the websites listed here.

US SUPPLIERS

YARN SUPPLIERS

Bluefaced Leicester
Wool2Dye4
6000-K Boonsboro Road
Coffee Crossing
Lynchburg
VA 24503
www.wool2dye4.com

Debbie Bliss
www.debbieblissonline.com

Fyberspates
www.fyberspates.com

Mez Crafts Rowan Yarns
www.mezscrafts.co.uk

Purl Soho
www.purlsoho.com

Rooster Yarns
www.laughinghens.com

Rooster & Fyberspates
Knitcellaneous
120 Acorn Street
Merlin,
OR 97532
www.knitcellaneous.com

Yarn Forward
www.yarnfwd.com

TUITION

Nicki Trench Workshops
Crochet, knitting, and craft workshops at all levels
Email: nicki@nickitrench.com

STOCKISTS

A.C. Moore
Stores nationwide
1-888-226-6673
www.acmoore.com

Hobby Lobby
Stores nationwide
www.hobbylobby.com

Jo-Ann Fabric and Craft Store
Stores nationwide
1-888-739-4120
www.joann.com

Knitting Fever
Stockists of Debbie Bliss, Noro, and Sirdar yarns
www.knittingfever.com

Knitting Garden
Stockists of Rowan yarns
www.theknittinggarden.com

Laughing Hens
Wool, patterns, knitting & crochet suppliers online
www.laughinghens.com

Love Knitting
www.loveknitting.com

Michaels
Stores nationwide
1-800-642-4235
www.michaels.com

WEBS
www.yarn.com

UK SUPPLIERS

The Berwick Street Cloth Shop
Linings and trimmings
14 Berwick Street
London W1F 0PP
+44 (0)20 7287 2881
www.theberwickstreetclothshop.com

Blue Faced Yarn Shop
H W Hammand & Co
The Croft Stables
Station Lane
Great Barrow
Cheshire CH3 7JN
www.bluefaced.com

Debbie Bliss Yarns
Designer Yarns
Units 8–10
Newbridge Industrial Estate
Pitt Street
Keighley
West Yorkshire BD21 4PQ
+44 (0)1535 664222
www.designeryarns.uk.com

Fyberspates
The Maintenance Room
The Nalder Estate
East Challow
Nr Wantage
Oxfordshire OX12 9SY
+44 (0)7540 656660
www.fyberspates.com

Ingrid Wagner
Giant crochet supplies
Studio 5
The Stone Barn
Kirkharle Courtyard
Kirkharle
Northumberland NE19 2PE
+44 (0)1830 540117
www.ingridwagner.com

John Lewis
Stores nationwide
+44 (0)845 604 9049
www.johnlewis.com

Love Knitting
www.loveknitting.com

Rooster Yarns
Laughing Hens online
Wool, patterns, knitting & crochet supplies
www.laughinghens.com
+44 (0)1829 740903

Rowan Yarns
Green Lane Mill
Holmfirth
West Yorkshire HD9 2DX
+44 (0)1484 681881
www.knitrowan.com

VV Rouleaux
Ribbons and trimmings
101 Marylebone Lane
London W1U 2QD
+44 (0)20 7224 5179
www.vvrouleaux.com

INDEX

ACKNOWLEDGMENTS

This book has been full of fun. Not being much of a horror fan, I was deeply surprised at how all the gory, disgusting characters evolved from deep in my psyche. Worrying!

I am much in debt to so many people, particularly Jill Holden, who with great reluctance eventually succumbed to the lure of the Scaries and got roped in to help enormously. Thanks to Beckie who just managed to try out the cobweb pattern before Ophelia was born; Sue Lumsden for pulling me out of a deadline hole; and to Sharon Young and Theo for adding some essential accessories; also thanks to Jo Mason for expertly styled glasses. Mum, thanks again for some great pattern checking; and to Roger Perkins and Christopher Hart for checking words and for some inspiration. Thanks also to many of my customers who have come along and supported me on my 'scary journey' and given me great tips and advice along the way.

Great support as ever from Pete Jorgensen, Cindy Richards, Marie Clayton, and all at Cico Books. And finally an enormous credit to Rob Merrett, the stylist. He really captured the essence and humor that I tried to put into the Scaries and made it a really fabulous book.